Beloved Uncle Hyacinthe

Father Alexis Wiehe

Translator: Rodney Philips

Clink
Street

Published by Clink Street Publishing 2021
Copyright © 2021

First edition.

Original Title: Bien-aimé tonton Hyacinthe
Original edition: © Editions du Lau, France 2016

ISBN:
978-1-913962-26-5 - paperback
978-1-913962-27-2 - ebook

In memoriam

Captain P.B. Garstin MC
Sergeant T. Varey
Lance-corporal H. Lutton
Private T. J. Barker
Private J. Walker
Private W.P. Young

of D Squadron. 1st S.A.S. Regiment,
who did not return from OPERATION GAIN,
France, 1944

Table of Contents

Preface

It is with much pleasure that I have accepted a quest from my nephew, Père Alexis Wiehe, to preface his book on our uncle Hyacinthe, my father's brother.

The family synergy of events, which has led to the writing of this book, was born after one of Hyacinthe's nephews had seen a documentary on the 'Red Berets', which commemorated the 70ᵗanniversary of D-Day in France. This moving movie, in which their regiment's chaplain is interviewed, has stimulated our family to honour the memory of Hyacinthe through a narrative book.

I have read Alexis's manuscript almost in one go, thrilled to see how successful he has been in sharing Uncle Hyacinthe's intimate journal from the day he left the family mansion of Labourdonnais and its garden, without looking back, dedicating himself entirely to the victory of Liberty. This journal ends abruptly on the day his squadron was parachuted at La Ferté-Alais in France, at the time when the Allied Troops landed in Normandy.

Alexis will move on with his narrative with the help of numerous letters found in the family archives and with that of numerous witnesses, chosen amongst those who knew our uncle in person.

All along I have much appreciated Alexis's delicate manner of retracing the events of our uncle's life, through the perspective of his love for his mother Antoinette and his beloved fiancée Eda,. Both have certainly been a very strong support for him during his ordeals.

For my part, I have to admit that I have not been very generous in my correspondence with my uncle when I was finishing my studies at the Seminary in France, at the time when Uncle Hyacinthe, paralyzed, was back in Mauritius after the war. However, I have kept a very precious testimony of him through one of his letters written to me. I understand that he went through a very hard time when, paralyzed and in pain, he thought that his life was no longer of any use and had no meaning. All his dreams had been wrecked, and whatever future was left, it was shattered by the weight of unbearable pains. In those days there was no proper medication apart from morphine, which had to be administered in great moderation.

It is during that period that Uncle Hyacinthe met a few people who helped him to understand that every instance of life had a great value for God, the One who had given him that life. To accept and offer his sufferings in communion with Christ's did not attenuate them but conferred them a greater value. Hyacinthe, gradually, as the sun illuminated our planet Earth, was in profound communion with all Masses, continually celebrated all over the world.

On this year 2016, when Uncle Hyacinthe would have reached his 100th birthday on 28th May, the descendants of Adrien and Antoinette Wiehe have gathered together on this very same day. Our family has assembled around the Eucharist in thanksgiving to Our Lord for having given us such an uncle, who leaves us such a testimony of an accomplished life.

I wish to thank Alexis, from the bottom of my heart, for the dedication and the great involvement he threw in this project, as well as all those who have actively participated in the retrieval of all information and archives necessary for its realization; they will recognize themselves.

Let me share with you the text engraved on the stele, which has been erected in honour of Uncle Hyacinthe, in the garden of Labourdonnais, near the pavilion where Hyacinthe lived till the end of his life.

IN HOMMAGE TO UNCLE HYACINTHE

WHO LIVED IN THE GARDENS
OF LABOURDONNAIS

WAR-WOUNDED IN 1944.

THROUGH HIS BRAVERY AND HIS HEROISM,

HE WAS AN EXAMPLE TO HIS FAMILY
AND FRIENDS.

HIS SUFFERING, HIS FERVENT FAITH,

HIS COURAGE, HIS HOLINESS,

HIS SWEETNESS, HIS HUMILITY,

MARK HIM AS AN ELITE

WORTHY OF PRAISES AND ADMIRATION.

HE LIKED TO BE SURROUNDED

BY TREES AND BIRDS,

IN HIS QUEST FOR THE ABSOLUTE.

Father J.J. Adrien Wiehe
Priest of the Diocese of Port-Louis
Mauritius

Foreword

In June 2014, the Wiehe family invited me to write a book about my great uncle Hyacinthe, my paternal grandfather's brother I thank them for their trust. This assignment has led me through a very beautiful adventure I would never have lived without this project. Most of all, it was a family adventure.

As I've been a priest in the diocese of Toulon, France, for quite many years now relations with members of my family remaining in Mauritius were quite limited owing to distance. But thanks to this book project, I had the opportunity to engage in beautiful and numerous exchanges with several of them, and the contribution of each has been precious and indispensable for me to move forward. I thank first and foremost my Dad for his support (and) Johann for his availability.

Several of my uncles and aunts have agreed to provide their testimony to this book , whether a written or an oral one. Although it has not always been possible for me to render textually what they narrated to me, I thank them for their confidence. I would not have been able to proceed to the end of this biography without the contribution of those who had followed uncle Hyacinthe all along.

I would also like to thank many other family members for their collaboration to this adventure. A special thank among others to Dominique who played a key role in the transmission of information and archives and above all to serve as a link between all of them.

Thanks finally to my two uncles, Adrien and Denis, whom I was delighted to see again in the context of this project., and with whom the exchanges have been (so)enriching.

In his journal, Hyacinthes wrote: *"The family, this institution to which we are so much attached in Mauritius, is an exceptional thing and one of the most beautiful that are given to us"*. This book has been the opportunity for me to verify this truth.

Moreover, this has been a literary adventure. As the initial work consisted in going deeply through the notes and mails written by Uncle Hyacinthe, I have been immediately struck by the quality of his pen. While writing his biography, I have tried to reach this high quality, and to write as well as he does; but I have to admit that I have not succeeded. This failure has the advantage of highlighting the numerous extracts from his notes and letters, which are published here.

This literary adventure has been reinforced by the reading of different reference books, which are indicated at the end of this present one, and allowed me to refine my search.

My investigations have also taken me towards a family historic adventure! I have been able to accede to very interesting documents, not only in the national archives of Mauritius, but also in the family archives that have been recently sorted out, as well as other sources. Through those documents, I have been able to travel in time, relive different captivating events, for example the landing of the first airplane in Mauritius, the atmosphere of Holy Sites in Palestine before the creation of the State of Israel, or, still more, the liberation of Paris in 1944.

Of course, testimonies from the family have all been priceless and captivating. However, I wish to evoke here the memory of Mrs Henaff, now deceased, whom I have had the joy of meeting, and of corresponding with, during several months. Mrs. Henaff spent all her life at La Ferté-Alais. But she was still an adolescent when Hyacinthe jumped by parachute near that little village on 4th July 1944. Having never forgotten all that had happened during that period of war, she has allowed me to better acquaint myself with the context of that time.

Finally, to write this book has been like going through a spiritual adventure. Thanks to Uncle Hyacinthe's writings and to his conserved personal belongings, I was edified by the quality of his interior journey. He has let himself be seized by an absolute Love, which took him to accept many sacrifices. He has sought to imitate Jesus-Christ, living a great intimacy with him, especially in the Eucharist, and thus finding his vocation in the offering of his sufferings in communion with his Lord.

"I realize more and more the spiritual value of sufferings", he wrote, *"as much for others as for myself, and what I desire above all for myself is to be able to accept the divine will whatever it may be. You will understand me if I tell you that the sufferings, as much the physical ones as the moral ones, that I have endured, especially these last few years, and which are still very present today, cannot be truly accepted except with a supernatural aid."*

Dear readers, it is a beautiful story that you are about to discover! I have told it as I could, with elements that are non-exhaustive, and within the short time allotted for its publication on 28th May 2016, in accordance with the family request.

I have tried to remain as objective as possible. However, when one writes, our inspiration is obviously marked by our personal, therefore subjective, experience too. To write Uncle Hyacinthe's biography, I have therefore been involved as a man, as a Christian, as a priest, as a Mauritian who left his native island to serve the Church of France.

In conscience, I think that I have done all my possible not to betray Uncle Hyacinthe's memory, and tried to be as close as possible to the reality of his life and of his message.

May this reading give the opportunity to everyone, whether a member of his family or not, to meet someone really worth being acquainted with.

During all this period of research and writing, I have been privileged to live a marvellous adventure! I am sure that it will not stop here, and that it will be, for you too, a source of inspiration, particularly with regards to the sense of suffering. Uncle Hyacinth is a witness who teaches us to grow in humility.

"Suffering", he wrote, *"which it would seem paradoxical at first sight to call a divine gift, is truly a great privilege: but how would we be able to accept it with only our human forces?"*

May the Holy Spirit, the force from on High, illuminate us, and guide our steps towards the path of peace.

Father Alexis Wiehe
11 February 2016

WIEHE FAMILY: Abridged Genealogy

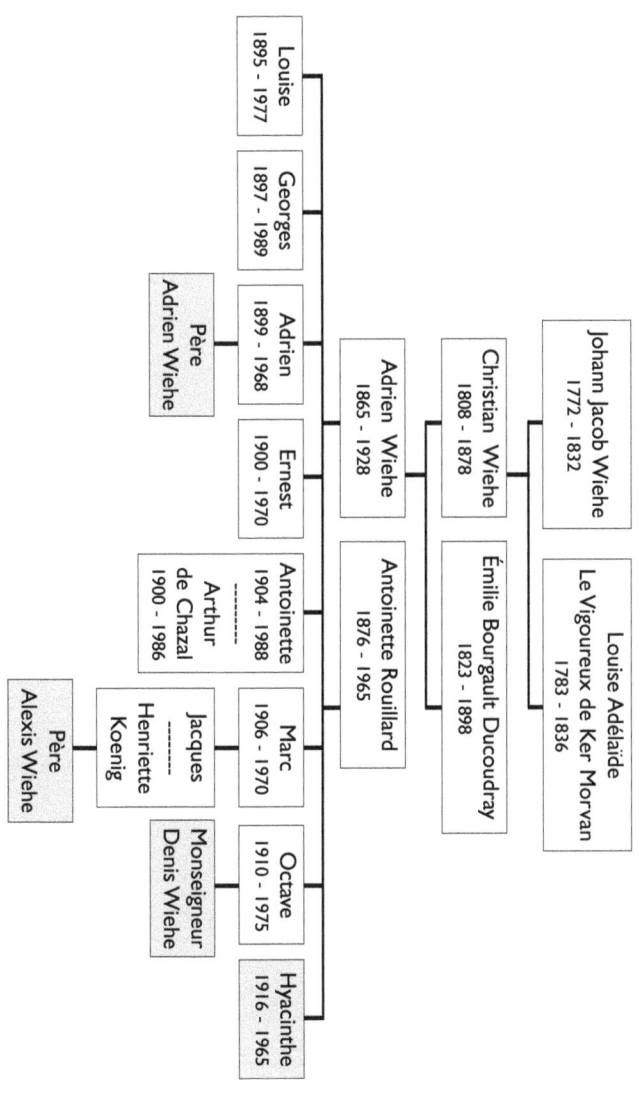

Louise 1895 - 1977

Georges 1897 - 1989

Père Adrien Wiehe

Adrien 1899 - 1968

Ernest 1900 - 1970

Adrien Wiehe 1865 - 1928

Christian Wiehe 1808 - 1878

Johann Jacob Wiehe 1772 - 1832

Louise Adélaïde Le Vigoureux de Ker Morvan 1783 - 1836

Émilie Bourgault Ducoudray 1823 - 1898

Antoinette 1904 - 1988

Arthur de Chazal 1900 - 1986

Antoinette Rouillard 1876 - 1965

Père Alexis Wiehe

Jacques -------- Henriette Koenig

Marc 1906 - 1970

Octave 1910 - 1975

Monseigneur Denis Wiehe

Hyacinthe 1916 - 1965

H Hour

28 May 1944. Another birthday that makes me turn back briefly on what is called a life journey, and muse upon the years that accumulate backwards, so numerous now. The fourth birthday now far from all mine , far from my country; a birthday still marked by the absence of everything which I am fighting for, of everything that should have some sense of happiness, some of that true happiness which, I believe, I should forget now . Will there be another 28 May for me? And if there should be one, will it not find me sitting once again in front of this notebook to put down a few poor hopes yearly and irrevocably destroyed?

Hyacinthe had retired for a short time in the silence of his room on this day of his twenty eighth birthday. He had taken up his pen while looking mechanically around this darkish room where his modest personal belongings were stacked. This day should have eased his face and broadened his smile, but he could not get rid of those gloomy thoughts that were obsessing him.

"Happy Birthday!" Those two words usually generated a simple and deep joy elating his soul. Alas! On this 28 May 1944, nothing was the same anymore. The slightest objects surrounding him evoked war: devised for battle or for camouflage, for killing or for self-defence... He sighed; this war was making him nauseous and provoked in him explosions of anguish and sadness, wafts of sad thoughts, chilling him as never before. Ah! How sweet was the time before the war, and how long and heavy this new part of his life!

He often experienced the urge to write a few words in this notebook that had been following him since his departure from Mauritius in 1941. He always felt much better once his feeling and his thoughts unloaded. His pen was like a faithful companion, a crutch on which to lean when he stumbled, a sort of secret remedy for keeping his ideas clear from losing his deep inner motivations.

He comforted himself with the thought that perhaps, one day, someone dear to him would share some parts of what he had seen and heard: that his mother or his brothers, his sisters or his fiancée would thus find out what he had endured, what he had gone through and observed, and share those numerous questions too often left unanswered.

He had experienced a certain sense of fulfilment for keeping a record of his exile, far from his beloved ones. But now, on this 28 May 1944, Hyacinthe had even lost the taste of writing and he was getting so tired of waiting. How numerous his delusions during those past years! To belong to a regiment, obey its orders, follow its instructions: all this had brought him a certain satisfaction, an unequalled sense of accomplishment once duty done.

But even then, that interior peace, that sweet and familiar serenity had disappeared. He was worn out by the coming and going rumours, by the incessant contradictory hearsays, by the loquacious forecasts, so often ill founded, which in the end was sapping all energy!

He hunted for the right words, flipping backward and forward these pages covered day in and day out with dark ink; in need of inspiration he preferred to browse back through his notebook and read over some extracts. He acknowledged the motions he had taken time to put down in writing; motions of troops or of seasons, surely, but mainly the numerous interior ones: those of a heart that had so often felt the need to open itself, to express itself by means of some ink and paper.

This 28 May 1944 was Pentecost Sunday. As usual, Hyacinthe had taken time to say his prayers. It was quite hard for him to get rid of this loneliness which, the more he let his thoughts wander off, the more grew so gloomily upon him. In the officers' mess, he met his fellows sitting at tables around several beers. He had already been wished a happy birthday earlier, but when they noticed such a dark expression on his face, his friends invited him to join them. And the conversation carried on around the same subjects: when will the landing take place? what would everyone do once the war over? Hyacinthe played the game as usual, but it was not natural for him to talk for hours in english, with individuals who had not known his pre-war life, who did not have the same cultural references as his. They were all in their twenties; some looked like young adolescents.

7 June 1944

The big Day has arrived! The grand invasion of Europe has started. I was discussing with a friend just yesterday morning, making conjectures as to the date of this great event; a motherent later, the radio announced: *"Allied forces have landed on the continent of Europe"*. Away, on the Normandy coast, out of countless ships from England men, tanks, canons, disembark by the millions. Disembark and run for assault: There, those soldiers from Great Britain and the United States, ruthless and unabated, are advancing and killing, but they kill and die too. *"The battle of France has started"*, says General de Gaulle.

Down here, we are still awaiting. Some time ago, two squadrons of the regiment have left for the South. They are perhaps already in France, or will be there soon. As for me, I am leaving with my squadron in two days and we shall soon follow the others on the continent, I think. At first it was decided that we would be parachuted in France one day before invasion; and then our mission was cancelled, as the risks of the first initiative would apparently be too perilous. While we wait for departure, our training carries on and intensifies. We are constantly in manoeuvre in the south of Darvel, in this beautiful countryside, resplendent with Spring. Everywhere, trees and bushes are covered with tender leaves, buds blooming, forming a pattern of ever changing greens. Or else, it is the rhododendrons which are adorning this greenery, like an orgy of exploding colors.

There are also all these little villages that we pass through, where we stop at the "pub" for a glass of beer, time permitting; villages that have their particular charm , but all so clean, so shiny. Nights spent in the barns, if possible, where the heat and comfort of hay are welcome; or else we sleep in nature; it does not feel too good in the woods when it rains, but one has to get used to it.

Now, I close this notebook for a long time, probably. Maybe, next time, if I feel like writing a few hasty notes, I shall be in a camp waiting for my departure for France, in occupied country, far behind the enemy lines. Or are these notes that I am writing presently the last ones?

Those notes that I write now ... are they the last ones?

This sentence, after more than 350 pages written over the course of three years, puts an end to Uncle Hyacinthe's confidences. The event, so much waited for, and anticipated during so many months, had arrived at long last! The Allies were landing in France! Once the news heard, his melancholy disappeared at once. It was as if someone, banging on his door, had come to get him out in the middle of the night.

A strange feeling took thence hold of Hyacinthe: it was like a sort of relief, melt with stress and excitement. A relief for not having to keep waiting anymore, yes, but also, like a shot of adrenalin rushing all over his being, grew the knowledge that danger was imminent now! He knew he would be exposing himself to serious risks.

From 27 April 1944, he belonged to the first S.A.S, *Special Air Service*, a special unit of the British Forces, also known as *'the Sabotage Parachutists*

In the British army, this regiment was subjected to the most stringent training. In order to better prepare the missions behind the enemy lines, they had to be apt to face the most extreme situations. There were twelve soldiers serving under the order of Captain Garstin: ten Englishmen, one Frenchman, and one Mauritian.

Often during their training, they jumped in tough conditions. In groups of six, they regularly marched tens of kilometres to stretch their endurance, to bear the wounds caused as much by the belts of their bags as by the uneven grounds. Carrying only one sleeping bag and light weapons, they departed for several days without money or food except for a few vitamin candies called '*tablets*': one for each elementary nutrition. They specialized themselves in overcoming the most daunting pitfalls : high walls, barbed wires, icy streams, deep ditches and ponds.

His companions had the opportunity to return to their house, their family, when they were on leave. During such times he envied them a little. Although it was a satisfaction for him to be in England, in a safe country, he noted down:

This satisfaction is obviously not comparable to that of my fellows for whom the word England sounds no more than 'HOME'.

Solitude was more intensely felt during those leave periods when most of his fellows went off, all happy to commute with their parents and friends. He took advantage of this time to go for walks through nature, whenever weather permitted. These solitary walks regenerated him in a particular way. He appreciated walking at his own leisure, breathing with full lungs, to better appreciate all various sceneries. In spite of the cold and humidity, he always marvelled at the beauty of nature.

Some months before, in the heart of winter, he had noted down his feelings:

"I love the countryside - even if I have only seen little now, and, given the actual season, I can't really see the extent of all its splendour. But I find that even winter reflects all its beauty. I don't want to speak of the charm, of the grace which everything is embraced with, each tree branch, each creation of man, when nature enwraps them with a white mantle. It would be commonplace to speak of this soft sweetness that is in every surrounding when snow appears, turning the lawns into an immaculate carpet , every single bush into a fairylike scenery, festooning the window sill, rounding off the corner of the fencing wall, adorning the old slate roof. No, what has struck me most with their powerful beauty because honest and sincere, are all those tall trees so well grouped, so well isolated, in this beautiful English countryside.

At this motherent, they have no foliage to adorn them, but what we see of them is their most beautiful part: it is their very soul: these huge blackened trunks, these tall branches, these thousands small ones, show themselves to us with all their energy and the marvellous flexibility of their gait, which make me revere them even more."

It is by means of this nature, which he was familiarising himself with, that he discovered also a new culture. As he walked through the United Kingdom, from the North of Scotland to the South of England, he had noted down some appreciations:

"Here and there, the same tranquil air, the same gentleness of the inhabitants, the same charm, in the same old stone dwellings, with their greenish slates, the same appearance of serene dilapidation in the old church. And there is particularly this unique English institution, the '*pubs*' which are neither coffee shops nor restaurants, nor bars, nor bistros: untranslatable word - and incomprehensible to the one who has not yet known any. How forget the names they display, always diversified, apart from a few old traditional names?

In the neighbouring village, there's the '*Stags and Hounds*' or the '*Horse and Trumpet*' or the '*Three Horse Shoes*' or the '*Manekton's Arms*', and others.

And now I want to speak of London where I landed a week after my arrival in England. London, centre of the British Empire, has, like all of us, more than all of us, donned its uniform: American soldiers, traffic restrictions, black-out, severe rationing in restaurants, the Eros of Piccadilly Circus invisible under its protective coat, military vehicles on the streets. And London, capital of the British Empire, also shows its scars, for, since a few years now, relentless, she is fighting: scars that one sees here and there, in the West End, in South Kensington, and deeper scars in the city – even in the region of the docks apparently.

But this aspect of war has not made her lose the congenial atmosphere of a big city, that she already possessed, I think. I have not been impressed by her blacked buildings, the lack of perspective in its streets. I was disappointed by the proportions of Piccadilly Circus; I have been shocked to see how the monuments were placed, irrespective of any axis, I have fulminated against days of thick fog, against days of icy wind. But I have liked, yes I like London and its atmosphere, not because of its superb abbey with its stone laces, not because of St Paul and its beautiful proportions, not because of the large river Thames, but because of a nondescript feeling.

When, after one month of leave in London, I came back again for a few days, I felt at home, everything seemed familiar. And also, in London,

I met my friends from Mauritius, those who are worth so much more than the once-a-time fellows whom we meet in the army. It was so good to be in Clavistella's mess at 10 Thurlor St., to be there with Mark, Duke and Camille, with John and Mike and the others. To bring up common memories, to share news of our country, to speak of those whom I can never mention anywhere. All this, as if those ante-war happy days were being replayed.

But now I have left all this behind. What is waiting for me, what is waiting for all of us, is quite hard to think of ! How many of us will come back from it? The Prime Minister said to Lord Kinsley that the press should prepare the British population to what should be happening next, keep it from excessive optimism regarding the price of victory, warn it against the enormous losses that our army is going to suffer in terms of human lives.

But who would dare to retreat from the effort that is demanded? Better still, who does not aspire to be part of those forces that are being trained for the final assault? I have not volunteered my application for any particular position where my knowledge of French would be of use: to be immediately dropped by parachute into France, be sent on reconnaissance, establish a liaison with those over there, in other words, anything that would be requested from me.

Since he had already sacrificed his life, he felt ready to offer himself for the liberation of France. He remembered the stories running in his family, which transmitted the love of France and of England, stories that united two different cultures which had often been otherwise opposed or confronted.

To participate in the liberation of France was an honour and a source of pride for Hyacinthe. In his view, a great nation was being humiliated and he was determined to defend it, even if he sometimes felt a sort of fear, an anguish mixed with some bad premonitions which he tried to evacuate by means of desperate appeals to his reason. Those fears rose in him like a chill shooting out of the depths of his still so young existence, but he tried to overcome them with all his power.

Is it because I lose confidence, I can't say! But right now, when I have to carry out a parachute drop, I am filled with an apprehension and an anguish that I find difficult to overcome. I am afraid, simply afraid.

Those feelings came to him regularly, and he did not know how to fight back those dark ideas that obsessed him:

Now is a Sunday that ends sadly, in spite of this beautiful Spring sun that enlightens all scales of greens in the trees, in spite of the birdsongs, in spite of nature's different aspects. All this should render me happy, should banish sad thoughts, warm up my soul. But no, neither sun nor festive nature can dissipate this mist that enwraps me like a shroud. Foreboding about what is going to happen, fears of what will be my fate?

A few days after having put a final stop to his notebooks - which was also an interrogation mark - more than ever came to Hyacinthe this question: *Shall I die? Are my days counted?*

He felt the need to write to his mother. One last letter to force himself to remain optimistic as to the outcome of the operations, to reassure those whom he loved so much.

16 June 1944

My very dear mother,

Yesterday I received good news about the family, in a long letter from Marc, which has pleased me greatly. I am happy to know that you were well by the time he wrote. When these few notes will reach you, I shall already be on the European continent. I dared not mention it to you myself, but the colonel told me yesterday that we were allowed to. You should not be alarmed if, after this letter, you have no news from me for a long time. I ask you to continue to write to me: although the letters will most probably reach me, I shall not be able to reply to them.

You will not even hear about my regiment in the press releases, and I cannot tell you what our role will be. Though our mission is difficult to accomplish, I depart with full confidence. I shall soon be back: I prefer to be honest with you, as I have always been my dear mother, rather than try to hide the truth from you. But I have to tell you once more: If what I do, or rather what I shall soon do, offers some dangers, I have reasons to be confident. I am also writing to Eda; I know that in spite of her anxiety she will not show her feelings; but I count on you to reassure her and give her courage.

I cannot write to the family: you will tell them all my affection. More than ever I shall be with you in thought and in prayer. And I am sure that I am right to say: See you soon!

I kiss you very tenderly,

Your son who loves you. H

A few days after this letter, the time had come for him and his companions. But this first mission nearly turned out to be the last. It had been agreed to jump near Brétigny-sur-Orge, in the Parisian region, where Resistance fighters were supposed to wait for them. If no light showed up at Brétigny, they would then have to continue to La Ferté-Alais.

The joy of seeing it all end was intertwined with a fear of the unknown. Up in the air, cold was difficult to endure. A shudder ran through his body, and he could not identify its source: was it the cold or his own anxiety?

A few words were exchanged between these youngsters. Some were swearing in order to decompress.

After verifying his material, Hyacinthe took out his rosary and held it tightly in his hand. He closed his eyes a few seconds while repeating this prayer so often said. He knew it by heart, but never had it sounded so earnest:

"Holy Mary, Mother of God, pray for us sinners now and at the hour of our death."

Now was the H hour.

D-day had launched the start of crucial days for the ultimate victory. D-day was the first landing day in Normandy. 6 June 1944: a date remembered in history books, such an important date in the great History, for it marked the start of the victory process. But how many days left before the Armistice of 6 May 1945? There would still be more tears to wipe, blood to shed, cruelties to face . And each day hid some H hours, as each soldier had his own hour. The hour at which he had to enter the stage, to throw himself entirely in an ultimate battle, without turning back, without expecting anything in return except to participate in the final victory, with the hope to stay alive.

During the course of this mission, almost everything turned out dramatically. The plane was hit by shots from the enemy: holes appeared in the floor, one of the reactors caught fire. With an heroic courage and a lot of cold-blood, the on-board mechanic succeeded in extinguishing the fire. The engine seemed to be faltering dangerously when it approached Brétigny.

The pilot thought that he was doing the right thing by letting the parachutists jump before attempting to save the plane, but the signals did not light up.

They learnt later that the Resistance fighters knew they were being watched by the enemy, and they had therefore given up going to the appointed place. There remained only one solution: retreat quickly to England! Thanks to the competence and intrepidity of the pilot, something unexpected took place. The plane made it to the first British airport and landed despite impossible conditions. A few days later, during a conference with the colonel, a large map of the Parisian region was opened. Some landmarks were chosen in the vicinity of La Ferté-Alais where they would be expected: the Juine River, the Étampes Route, and the village of Villeneuve ...

Hyacinthe and his fellows memorized all those information. This was a crucial time. The Nazis has already begun to raid London with their famous V1, aiming first at demoralizing Allied troops whilst slowing the armament manufacture.

Moreover, though the Allied were progressing their way into France, they met strong resistance from the enemy not ready to surrender that easily.

The second take-off for a new mission was like a new departure, a new H hour. In the black night, the twelve young men succeeded to jump near La Ferté-Alais, 50 kilometres south of Paris, and assembled around their captain instantly. Without wasting time, they buried their parachutes and immediately started to execute the orders they had been given.

Within a few days, and without much difficulty, they sabotaged a German train, exploded large ammunition dumps, and returned straight back to England by a plane that had fetched them.

Given the numerous risks, adrenaline rose, tension soared. Without taking time to recover, they had already to prepare for the next mission. The battle was intensifying and spreading its wings, there was therefore no time to waste! The war was far from being won!

As German reinforcements were arriving in France, risks increased tremenduously! Conscious of the stakes, Hyacinthe's S.A.S. regiment was assigned an even more perilous mission. It consisted in remaining in France for a month in order to sabotage all the airports to the west of Paris.

Before this grand departure, he felt a big contraction through his heart. He would have so much loved seeing his brothers again for a loud guffaw. Or having Eda at his side, to take her in his arms, and tell her how much he loved her. He thought about his mother, he knew that she was praying for him, and this comforted him. He had never been able to get rid of that fear that often took him by surprise, knotting his stomach. How soothing for him, then, to wander through the English countryside, to stretch his legs and cleanse his mind.

There only remained a few hours before take-off, and his last walk provided him a great sense of well-being, that helped him to fight the rising pressure. Outstretching his legs, he let himself go, whilst nursing so many precious memories and dreams!

His minded wandered back on his walks at Labourdonnais with his brothers and cousins, his excursions in the North when he was at 'Sans Souci'. He could feel under his shoes the solid earth that summer had recently dried. Here and there, rose some muddy puddles that he tried to avoid.

He kept his eyes riveted on all this beauty, in order to refresh his mind , to fight against those calamities threatening his thoughts. He had to fight hard within himself in order not to give in to those dark forebodings: he hummed some tunes, and few birds echoed. Their chirps took him back to Mauritius. It was good to walk under the sun.

It was not a long hike, certainly, but there was nothing better than those few steps to feel lighter and to evaluate the price of living. Hyacinthe could not measure the importance of his steps, of those simple steps, before getting into the plane. The last steps before a grand mission. The last steps before engaging in a new combat. His last steps.

During the night of this 4 July, the H hour had come once again for twelve young men among hundreds of thousands more. Most of them did not survive this ultimate operation. But who cares about wartime data and statistics! Behind each uniform there was a person, a human being, with a singular history, a secret life. The lines which follow retrace the itinerary of one of them. He was praying fervently in that plane propelled into the night, carrying the destiny of these youths.

Mauritian Roots

July 1916. World War 1 was raging in Europe. The Battle of the Somme was particularly bloody. The Battle of Verdun had marked the minds, just as the air strikes on London on 13 June of the same year. Bleeding all over, the world was on fire. The map of Europe was being wiped out, later to be modified.

In the arms of his mother, a newborn was wailing. Barely one month old, he comforted himself in the arms of his mother, who was sitting on the veranda of the House of Labourdonnais, in the tropical serenity, far, very far from the atrocities that were tearing this world apart. A fragrance of mango perfumed the atmosphere, and the sweetness of the season enveloped nature in a beautiful aura of light.

The child listened to the birds' songs, amid the carefree shouts of his brothers and sisters playing, all the while slowly numbed by the soft whispers of his mother's prayers.

A few steps away from the house, the agricultural employees moved to and fro. The sugarcane harvest was ready to start, and , as every year, a particular ritual was being performed everywhere, rallying the Mauritian population quite significantly. The sugarcane fields were blooming, their flowers having already covered, as in a tapestry, a great part of the island with an ochre mantle.

The volcanic rock, which in the past had covered all the island, turned once a year into a huge flower garden at the harvest season.

This child in his mother's arms was named John Baptist Hyacinthe Wiehe. He took the first name from his maternal grandfather, who was then 74 years old, and whose strength was slowly declining. In the English colonies, as in the United Kingdom, the last name and not the first one, was the customary name.

Greek mythology tells the story of Hyacinthe, a handsome young man who died by accident. Out of his blood, flowers would bloom. A hyacinth is a flower belonging to the most beautiful bulbous ones that are still cultivated nowadays.

A hyacinth is also a precious stone with red, orange or brownish red hues. What a strange forename, synonymous with a flower and a precious stone!

But in the Catholic religion the forenames were chosen above all in reference to saints. Saint Hyacinthe (1185-1257), a Dominican priest in Poland, founded many convents in Russia, Lithuania, and in Poland. In the course of his missions, he travelled over most of Northern Europe: Sweden, Norway, and Denmark. After his canonization in 1594, his first name was given later to a town in Canada, a street in Paris, and even to a basilica in Chicago. He is invoked as the Patron Saint of Lithuania and apostle of the North.

It is also in the North, but in the North part of..... Mauritius, that this John Baptist Hyacinthe Wiehe, whom we see resting in the arms of his mother, was dwelling...

A beautiful flat land stretches from the chain of mountains to Grand Baie. The Labourdonnais estate is situated near the villages of Piton and Poudre d'Or, Mapou and Plaines des Papayes, in the parish of Pamplemousses.

It is there, in the church of St. Francis of Assisi, that we find Paul and Virginie as related in Bernardin de St. Pierre's famous book.

There is no trace of these illustrious youngsters who loved each other so much, but nowadays we can find, in the old parish graveyard, the tombs of Hyacinthe's ancestors, both on the paternal and maternal sides.

Since many generations back, the Wiehe family had taken roots in this part of the island, next to the famous botanical garden, well-known for its rare and very diversified species, for its tall tropical trees, its spices, and its gigantic water lilies!

On 1 February 1916, Hyacinthe's grandparents celebrated their golden anniversary in the church of Pamplemousses, which is still the oldest church on the island. The Wiehe family has safely preserved the blessing allocution that Father Malaval had given on that occasion:

«Isn't it therefore a striking special trait of divine providence that brings you back to the same altar, witness of your first vows on 1 February 1866? And the highest of heavenly favours is that you are here, surrounded by the numerous, by the most brilliant, crown of children, grandchildren, relatives and friends, all equally happy to share in your happiness, as well as in your joyful thanksgiving. Most of them will soon share with you the angels' banquet, before sitting at your sides, around the long family table. What a good example this is! How we should wish it to be followed by a greater number of our good Mauritian families!»

In the month of July 1916, France was introducing the summer time. But in Mauritius teatime bell had rung and the family had instantly assembled in the veranda for the daily *rendez-vous*.

Some cousins visited, unannounced. News were exchanged about each and everyone, current events were commented on ....

Amid diverse information, the local press reported some echoes of the distant war in a trivial way, as if they were all of equal importance: horse racing was postponed due to bad weather, the two cinemas of the island, Cinema Hall and Luna Park, proposed their movies at 50 cents, 25 cents, or 15 cents; ship arrivals, together with their merchandise, were announced.

One could also read, higgledy-piggledy, press releases of all sorts, ranging from notifications of engagement to that of a lost dog. And most of the newspapers posts showed that for the subscribers in general, time had stopped in Mauritius, in this small rock lost in the middle of the Indian Ocean, almost five times smaller than Corsica, fifteen times smaller than Britanny ... The South East trade winds blowing over it took the sugar cane fields into a dance, dragging towards the ocean the little local rumours.

The newborn was sleeping against his mother's breast as night fell. The children did not stop running around. Later, the youngest one would soon join them in that cheerful family atmosphere.

Hyacinthe, latest member of a family of nine children, was born on the 28 May 1916, the day on which the United Kingdom inaugurated the first flight of the British fighter-jet, 'Sopwitch Triplan'.

In July 1916, Boeing launched its very first airliner. In Mauritius, no plane had landed before, and no one could think that this would ever happen. To forecast that, one day, by tens of hundreds, these planes would take thousands of tourists, in search of sun and exoticism in the Indian Ocean, would be a fantasy as incredible as a science-fiction novel.

Light-years away from any continent, the Mauritian population felt far from everything, and believed that it would always be so. Few Mauritians travelled. To travel was a luxury because, on the one hand, one needed time to go on long journeys by ship and on the other hand, needed to have the proper means to afford the trip fare and stay in the large European cities.

But every Mauritian carries deep inside his genes one of his ancestors' travel on which to rely on.

This island, which was uninhabited during many centuries, had started to be populated on a permanent basis when the French decided to settle there in 1715. Over time, the settlers had landed after a long and somehow risky journey.

Every Mauritian can claim an ancestor who had once taken up this challenge, or else been submitted to a forced exile. In all the Mauritian families, the genealogical tree is like an uprooted, then transplanted tree, which has faced the difficult tropical context, the somehow trying atmosphere of a new social ecosystem, so fragile and so much different from the one they had left behind. Moreover, every Mauritian bears in him a dual sense of belonging , like an imprint of several cultures - the one of the distant origins and the one developed on the island, in the midst of sugarcane fields.

In order to know a little more about Hyacinthe Wiehe, and to better follow his itinerary, it is without doubt useful to reconstitute the family context in which he grew up, and the cultural heritage that shaped him.

We are all marked by a culture, but also by history and geography. To describe the geography of Mauritius is relatively easy. Everyone would be able to recapitulate the landscape of his childhood, the neighbourhood, and the street lines, the gardens and the houses, everything that leaves an imprint on us. Does not the nostalgia of childhood hide in tastes and smells, in everything that our senses have memorized?

History and culture are more complex realities, and it would be risky here to try to analyse its constituent parts. It would be a daring venture to try to decrypt one's life, merely on the basis of its family history and culture.

Geography, culture and history are exterior data that influence the interior being. We receive them without choosing. We absorb them without being aware of it. They form us more than we think. They influence our way of being and thinking and the majority of our choices, as well as our position on circumstances which we are confronting.

Hyacinthe was of European origin.

His ancestor, Johann Jacob Wiehe arrived in Mauritius in 1792, at the age of 20, sent by his father, a trader from Copenhagen. At that time, Denmark had developed some commercial ties between Europe and India; and Mauritius, thence named Ile de France, was a home port, a quite ideal one for the trade.

Johann Jacob did not foresee the necessity to settle in the Indian Ocean, but love governed his destiny. In 1801, he married Louise Adelaide Le Vigoureux de Ker Morvan, whose family originated from Brittany and had settled on the island circa 1720, at the time of the very first French establishments in Mauritius.

Johann Jacob integrated the close circle of the French and Catholic landed gentry, which seems quite a feat for a man of German and Lutheran origin.

Between 1803 and 1820, ten children were issued of their wedlock, henceforth the first Mauritian Wiehe born on the island.

In 1810, The English conquered Ile de France which they renamed Mauritius - Ile Maurice in French – from the name given to it centuries ago by the Dutch, in honour of Maurice of Nassau, Prince of Holland.

The conquest of the island by the British played in favour of Johann Jacob who had never renounced his Danish origin. The English did not trust the French settlers, then the majority population on the island, most of whom nurtured a certain anglophobia. They tried their best therefore to seek the support of people who would be quite ready to establish a link between the inhabitants of French origin and the new English administration. Johann Jacob fitted perfectly into this role. He therefore contributed actively to the economic and social life during this new phase of the history of Mauritius, henceforth under the British flag.

Having grown relatively rich, his industrial and port-related commerce was situated for the most part in Port-Louis, the capital, where he owned shipyards, warehouses and several land properties and houses.

But in the years 1830, the island went through a serious economic crisis, and the Wiehe family was not spared by bankruptcy. The social unrest around the abolishment of slavery in 1835, and above all, the sudden death of the head of family, Johann Jacob, in 1837, were premonitory signs of worse things to come for a family that had barely settled in Mauritius.

To top it all, the Wiehe were shaken by a tragedy in 1836. The "*Doncaster*" was wrecked off the coast of South Africa, during a journey between Mauritius and Europe.

Among the passengers who perished were several members of Johann Jacob's family, namely his wife, three of his daughters, one son-in-law, and four grand-children. The Wiehe branch henceforth found themselves both fatherless and motherless, at a relatively young age (between 16 and 37 years).

Christian, the third of the six children of Johann Jacob, was one of the few to marry a Mauritian lady of French origin, most of his brothers and sisters having married English partners, or English descendants. Some of them left the island to live in Europe.

Christian, Hyacinthe's grandfather, took up the paternal torch, and ambitioned to reverse his father's bad luck, to prosper where the latter had failed.

He was in partnership with one of his brothers, with whom he had developed commercial activities of no great importance. In 1839, his marriage with Emilie Bourgault Ducoudray marked an important turning point. Thanks to the support of his in-laws, Christian found the necessary resources to launch himself into business again. He distanced himself from his brother, and succeeded in settling his home in a sustainable manner on a estate in the north of the island, known in the past as Bois Rouge, spread over 1,400 acres.

Christian Wiehe's father-in-law had bought back this property as well as some neighbouring sugar cane properties: Forbach (744 acres), Mon Repos (938 acres) and La Caroline (435 acres), as a result of which, the total estate formed a large property of 3,717 acres (about 15 square miles), named 'Labourdonnais' in memory of the most illustrious governor of Ile de France.

While the island was now under British rule, how daring to name a property with reference to a great French character who embodied a recent, but definitely bygone, past! This detail illustrates well the inner freedom Christian advocated towards the colonial power, and confirms his successful integration into the ecosystem where the French and English cultures cohabited rather peacefully.

For the anecdote, in 1812 the English favoured this cohabitation by creating the oldest hippodrome of the South Hemisphere at Champs de Mars in Port-Louis, in order to assemble English and French around horse-racing: a true success!

Christian was bilingual, and moved around both circles of French-origin gentry and new settlers of English-origin. His library contained many books ordered from Europe, on the subjects of History and Politics, but also of Agriculture, Architecture, as well as practical writings and books on Theology.

Attached to the faith of his fathers, but immersed in a Catholic environment by his wife and by the Mauritian context, Christian decided not to have his children baptized but rather leave them the choice when they would be adults. Quite unique at a time when one was more preoccupied with the soul's salvation than nowadays.

Marguerite Le Juge de Segrais, one of his granddaughters, gave evidence in her diary:

"My grandfather was Danish. Christian was a very distinguished man, related to the King of Denmark, he was protestant; my grandmother Émilie Bourgault du Coudray was Catholic, she was free to practise her religion but he had said to his wife: «The children will choose when they will be twenty.» How could my grandmother agree to that! It was certainly not without remorse as her children were not baptized.»

The British Empire was establishing itself without prejudice to the French culture which continued to permeate the life of Mauritians originating from France. This, in the middle of the Indian Ocean, created a unique microcosm of its kind, enriched by the arrival of Indian workers, called «engagés» (contractual workers). The latter came to replace the former slaves in the fields.

Above all, on his vast agricultural property, Christian developed the cultivation of sugar cane, the island's main industry since the legislation of 1825, which ruled the export of sugar from the colonies to Europe. Mauritius became the seventh world producer of sugar in the years 1840.

Christian ventured himself also in ornithology, horticulture, zoology, agronomy. He devoted a special passion to the culture of tropical fruits, and especially mangoes. A famous orchard was planted on his property, which continues to feed food lovers to this day. The sugar factory of Labourdonnais took advantage of the industrial boom of the island but also from the investment and know-how of Christian Wiehe, who erected a magnificent house on his domain, which in the end was know as "The Château". In the colonial style of creole habitats, with its large verandas, it gained a reputation, in that period, as one of the most beautiful in the island, surrounded by a luxuriant garden and situated at the end of a broad alley bordered with Intendance trees, those majestic trees that spread their branches and roots around.

All along the centuries, depending on the whims of cyclones which, at regular intervals, tested the island's resistance, its vegetation evolved. However, right after the construction of the house of Labourdonnais, the garden benefited from the tropical climate. Everything that was planted there rapidly embellished the surroundings, turning the yard of the château into a gallery of sculpted wood, a charming sort of choreography in the wind, an oasis of colors and perfumes, right in the middle of sugarcane fields.

Through the development of the domain of Labourdonnais, it was a whole family that rooted itself permanently on the island. Christian died in 1878, leaving to his eight children and all his descendants, an enchanting life and a prosperous enterprise of 500 acres, 40 mules, 60 oxen, as well as a splendid mansion, a unique orchard, an exceptional aviary, a vast deer park ...

He had succeeded in taking up the challenge his father had left him: to establish himself in Mauritius.

At his death, his son Henry became administrator of Labourdonnais. Then, a few years later, Adrien, last son of Christian and brother of Henry, took over the lead of the family domain.

At 29 years old, Adrien married Antoinette Rouillard in 1894. She was 18 years old, and issued from an old French and Catholic family, settled on the island in the seventeenth century, before the Wiehe's arrival.

The couple lived part of the year at Phoenix, on the high plateau, between Curepipe and Quatre-Bornes. But

Labourdonnais remained the family reference, the dearest dwelling home for all, the rallying point of all the generations where they stayed several months each year.

As administrator of the property, Adrien was constantly active, bearing on his shoulders the weight of an enterprise inherited from his father and which earned a living for a great number of Mauritian families.

A motorcar enthusiast, he was the first one to own one in Mauritius, and became a member of the Automobile Club of Mauritius in 1918. His membership card has been archived, bearing no. 009 and the mention: Ordinary Member.

The invention of the automobile being still recent, the roads and infrastructures were not very well adapted. The majority of Mauritians still travelled by train or horse drawn carriage.

Hyacinthe, the last child, attracted the affection and admiration of his brothers and sisters. Louise was 21 years old at his birth. Her older brothers, Georges and Adrien, aged 19 and 17 then, were preparing to follow their father. Ernest was 16 years old and was chosen to be Hyacinthe's godfather, while his sister Antoinette was his godmother at 12 years old. Marc, 10 years old and Octave, 6 years old, were the closest in age and were going to draw their little brother into their games.

While growing up, Hyacinthe had an interest in everything and asked many questions, taking advantage of a privileged family context, like a little prince immersed in the others' affection. He got familiar with the staff going back and forth in the house, in the kitchen, or else in the garden.

Quite bad-tempered from his tender childhood, he thus expressed his need of attention and his great sensitivity. Often, the children's jaunts ended in little crisis that surprised everyone, whether at Phoenix or at Labourdonnais,

This family domain marked him deeply and would remain his domain all his life: his playground, his hermitage, and his hiding place. There, more than anywhere else, he learnt to be filled with wonder, to contemplate the beauty of nature, to discover all the nuances of the surrounding atmosphere, bathed in sunlight and birdsongs. Like a fish in the sea, he enjoyed long promenades through the orchard or in the park, hunting for the best hiding places, and the trees that bore the best fruits, discovering flowers with all their nuances of scents.

When he reached the age to go to school, Hyacinthe entered the Père Laval College, where he benefited every day of a religious instruction which, on Friday, took place in the chapel with the exposition of the Blessed Sacrament.

The School year lasted from beginning of January to Easter, then from the Quasimodo Sunday to end of July, and finally from beginning of September to mid-December. Classes were in the morning from ten to noon, then from 1 pm to 3,30 pm. His school reports, which have all been archived, witness to his teachers' satisfaction, as much for his behaviour as for his performance as a studious child.

His soul revealed itself in his oldest letters, written with his childish hand. He had gone on a trip to Paris, and among the few missives addressed to his family, the following one is surprising:

«*Monday 14 May 1923*
My dear grandmother,
I think of you very much, I want to see you very much. I have a notebook of sacrifices, I note them down every day. We have changed apartment. I have been to Suresnes by boat the other day, it was fun. I went to the market. I have been to the roulettes and I won a small cat on Thursday. I went to Châtelet, and I had much fun. For the first time, I went to confess at Easter. It made me happy and since then, I am more reasonable, I am almost never angry, I send you a big kiss. Hyacinthe.»

Quite surprising Uncle Hyacinthe's first letter, at a time when he was not yet 7 years old! We notice his usual childish temperament, who liked to have fun. But, most probably, he was already learning good reflexes. By going to confession for the first time, he experienced God's grace. Usually he suffered from uncontrollable outbursts Yet, he noticed that confession helped him to better master himself. His interior virulence was disarmed by the kindness of God, the sweetness of His mercy, His loving strength.

We also learn that he owned a notebook on which he wrote his small sacrifices deliberately performed, thus manifesting the desire to improve himself. Of what sort of sacrifices could it be, for a child of 6 years old?

These famous notes no longer exist, but we can suppose that they may have consisted in a few food deprivation, or some acts of humility and efforts imposed upon himself.

At that time, this kind of spirituality was noticed in a child who was living in Paris. Among the objects left by Hyacinthe at his death, a relic of the said child lets us think that he had heard of that child whose canonization was expected, and that he would surely have prayed for his intercession.

Guy de Fontgalland was not yet quite well known at that time, but immediately after his death, on 24 June 1925, following a diphtheria, thousands of people, in France and around the world, invoked the intercession of that 11-year-old child. His mother wrote a short biography that was edited at 100,000 copies in France, and translated in 13 languages.

Very young, Guy sought to imitate Jesus and had an intimate relationship with him. Every day, he offered small sacrifices to please Him and received Holly Communion earlier than children of his age. He did not seek the limelight by extraordinary ways but manifested an authentic charity by protecting the weak, by forgiving easily, and avoiding to criticize others.

From all continents a large number of people, of all conditions, wrote to attest blessings received through Guy's intercession.

Obviously Hyacinthe did not know Guy at that time, and yet it would seem that they were alike on certain points. His little heart learnt love, self conquer, self forgetfulness, so as to fully devote himself to others.

The «vie de château « procured him a good education and good manners; the school life awakened his intelligence and his curiosity, thus favouring his self-realization . However, this fresh faith was important for Hyacinthe, orientating him towards the taste of God, the sense of good, the virtues of sacrifice. He did his first Communion on 6 May 1924.

Another time, he travelled at the age of ten, this time to Reunion Island, where thermal stations had developed in the island height, namely at Cilaos .

In the letters he wrote during this trip, we are quite amused to read the description of premises, or some funny episodes that sounded important to him. He was already very observant, and full of humour; not a single event around him escaped him. He had given some signs of fervour and piety before, however he remained also limited by his age, and spoke in one of his letters about a morning mass that had seemed to him 'quite long'

Besides these two voyages by ship, to metropolitan France and to Reunion, Hyacinthe's life followed roughly the ordinary course of that of all Mauritian children of his milieu. The family life filled him with joy, be it with his brothers and sisters or with his cousins who formed quite a gang .

During entire afternoons the little troop could vanish in nature, between the orchard and the great garden, between the intendances lane and the ponds.

Little by little, as he grew to know better his cousins, Hyacinthe bonded especially with Yves Rouillard of the same age as him, and who became his great friend.

He also loved Yves's sister, Eda, who often joined in their games. In their innocence, they often wondered about what they would do when they would grow up.

Choosing

Hyacinthe encountered a first ordeal at the death of his father in 1928, when he was only twelve years old. This was probably a blessing.

Faced with death, he discovered the sadness of those who wept, and felt the absence of the one who had left this Earth. But by confronting this reality so closely, he also took note of the vanity of this passing world. Everything passes. We pass. Questions dwelt in his mind without being able to take shape. What was the meaning of this life, what battle was to be fought, what was that call that resounded inward, unable to find a salutary path towards its realization? His sister Louise was devastated by their father's death and had to be admitted into a home for appropriate treatment.

His mother Antoinette was very attentive to each, but nutured a special affection for her youngest. As she cared for him with great tenderness, Hyacinthe was edified by the quality of her faith and of her Hope at the time of her bereaved widowhood.

All brothers and sisters had grown closer to each other since the death of their father. They were respectful towards their mother who instilled both sweetness and a natural authority. She knew how to handle her household and her children with an iron grip in a velvet glove. Over and above everything that she had been able to transmit to the Wiehe family, over and above her virtues, her culture and talents, she had, most of all transmitted a strong faith!

This so precious Faith had always ruled in the family but never with such fervour, such depth and such coherence.

Antoinette was born on a 7 October, Feast of Our Lady of the Rosary, in a practising Catholic family. All who knew her appreciated her simplicity, her culture, and especially the weight of her faith. She had been particularly influenced by the testimony transmitted by her parents, and mostly edified by her sister Caroline, who had joined a convent in France, henceforth being known as Mother Marie-Paul.

Hyacinthe had not known his aunt Caroline as he was around three or four years old by the time she left Mauritius, but she was quite a character who had impressed all by her piety, by her zeal both in announcing the Gospel and in devoting herself to the destitutes. Tradition recollects her as having been a very stimulating person, challenging each and every one – even a bit too directly, at times.. Though those who felt a little bit affected by this side of her character did not deny the fact that they were impressed by her total self abnegation with regards to others around her.

Since her parents had opposed her desire to take the religious orders, she had chosen initially to live in Mauritius as a religious lay, spending a lot of time visiting the destitutes, catechizing the children within the poorest and most remoted villages.

Enlivened by a great devotion to the Sacred Heart, as well as to St. Joseph, whom she invoked constantly, she used to travel quite long distances by train or by carriages just for the sake of Communion to the body of Christ.

At the time of her departure for France, everyone thought that this voyage was only motivated by her fragile health, which needed treatment. However during that voyage, seizing the opportunity of a stop in transit, she wrote to her parents to announce that she would never come back in order to answer a call for the religious life.

Mother Marie-Paul took part in the foundation of the 'Order of Little Maids of Christ the King' which no longer exists today. Deceased on the 11 October 1939, in her 53rd year, she had written before dying: *«Now that death touches me so near, I understand, I affirm, that the highest summit of perfection is total surrender.»*

Hyacinth moved from his school institution. On 9 December 1930, Père Laval College closed owing to a shortage of priests, and he was admitted into the Royal College of Curepipe. He was fourteen years old and one would not have been surprised to hear him express a desire to turn to priesthood. Perhaps he had questioned himself about such a a call. Indeed, he attended Sunday Mass, knew some priests who were close to the family, had gathered testimonies of certain Mauritians in his circle who were orienting themselves towards priesthood.

In 1928, three Mauritians were ordained : Leon Leclezio, Guy Le Juge de Segrais, and Jacques Giraud – this was an absolute record in the history of the local Church

Others, such as , Alexis Koenig or Henri Vigoureux.

were completing their formation.

At first , no serious question dwelt in Hyacinthe's mind on the subject of the sacerdotal vocation. His adolescence was marked rather by the marriage of his brothers and sisters. In 1923, his brother Georges had married May Rouillard, the sister of Yves and Eda. Adrien was married in 1928. Hyacinthe thus witnessed how all his brothers and sisters had found their soul mate. He observed all procedures preceding a marriage.

A little later, between his 17th and 22nd year, every year there was at least one wedding or the arrival of a baby. He thus was a prime witness to the birth of families.

From the first moments of meeting to the official presentation, from the announcement of marriage to its preparation; from its celebration to the apparition of the first children. All this marital procedure unfolded under his eyes: the natural unfolding, the inevitable budding of love that appears, then opens, ultimately concretizing into a lifetime commitment, in the responsibility of a parental vocation. Hyacinthe knew that this was what he could expect. But during his adolescence, questions competed with each other with more and more intensity. He read a lot, looked for answers to those secret questions. He prayed often, accompanied his mother to mass, confessed regularly.

Though his family stayed quite often at Labourdonnais, they actually moved from Phoenix to Floréal, and in this new house he got closer to his mother.

He felt responsible for her, whereas his brothers and sisters were progressively leaving the family home. Mother and child had often the opportunity to be on their own together, around a cup of tea or a meal, and their exchanges were profound, ranging from philosophy to theology, always punctuated by a great humour that consolidated their complicity.

These essential conversations helped Hyacinthe to build up his character, to grow into adulthood, even if he was not yet decided as to what his future would be. He spoke willingly to his mother about what he was doing with his friends, of what attracted him or rebuked him in general - particularly in the Mauritian society . She had become his confident, but a highly respected one. Never did she intrude into his secret garden; with delicacy, she did not pry into his feelings, nor did she bring up questions on which he did not want to venture.

As a child, he had learnt to make some small sacrifices to better himself, or else to favour deprivation so as to improve himself. Though he carried on practising those virtues, he often wondered about how far he would go. He had a feeling that life could have a meaning only if it was entirely offered. To offer everything, yes, but how? What for? Who for? It seemed to him that he was subjected to his environment's notion of offering: for a spouse and children, for a professional skill, for his country, like everybody else. However, owing to the books that he devoured he kept on dreaming of adventure. He wanted to risk his life, affront dangers, to reach the extremity of his limits.

Among the heroes who marked his youth during that period of his life, there were many aviators who had tried to beat world records in speed or distance.

Like many youths of his age, he would have dreamt to be a pilot too and to measure himself against big challenges. This dream never left his mind and even amplified on the occasion of the first airplane landing in Mauritius on 10 September 1937.

Hyacinthe was 17 years old then. The event was a premiere for this island lost in the middle of the ocean. The only way to communicate with neighbouring islands or with faraway continents was nothing else but by ship. The development of the Mauritian economy had benefited from maritime liaisons that favoured transits in Mauritius for commercial purposes.

Before the appearance of aerial transports in the island, the simple fact of living in the middle of the Indian Ocean conveyed to its inhabitants a strong feeling of being far away from everything, of being isolated, even forgotten by all. On certain world maps at the beginning of the twentieth century, Mauritius was not even represented: it seemed so insignificant, lost in the mass of oceans and continents!

The landing of the first airplane that had taken off from Reunion, less than 200 kilometres away, constituted an extraordinary event! Those present there would never forget it! And on that day, Hyacinthe was one of the privileged few who waited patiently, two steps away from the sea, until the first signs were heard. First a distant rumbling, this sound of motor that resounds more and more distinctly. All lifted their hands high in the air, hanging on to the strange buzzing sound that invaded the atmosphere, to try to be the first one to catch the sight of the approaching airplane. Then, arose shouts as well as hands stretched-out pointing towards this strange bird that was emerging at the horizon.

Among Uncle Hyachinte's belongings, many photos of this historical event have been preserved. However, all those present at that motherent kept each and every detail in their mind as if printed forever ! The chosen landing site for this grand *première* was an open ground in Mont Choisy, nowadays a public beach, planted and landscaped.

If many young men dreamt of flying, one had to be pragmatic, and content with what profession was locally available. With his artistic fibre, his sensitivity and his lively intelligence, Hyacinth eyed Architecture seriously. His grandfather Christian, the erection of his big family mansion, designed to resist cyclones and various ferocious weather conditions, were sources of great interest to him.

After completing school, he was therefore admitted at Boullé-Lagesse, one of the few, if not the sole, architectural firms existing on the island at that time. In reality, none of the two partners, neither Max Boullé nor Marcel Lagesse, had a real architectural formation, but they were both artists and had acquired rudimentary notions of architecture. Later, Schaub would bring to the cabinet more professional expertise.

Hyacinthe worked his best while pursuing the normal life of a Mauritian of his age and of his social environment, that is, extraordinarily well-balanced and fulfilling. He saw a lot of his cousins and friends who organised several outings at sea or different excursions in the heart of nature. No hotel existed then and they could thus enjoy at will , like little princes, all the splendours of the island.

They explored the coast, moving from bungalow to bungalow. Those houses, directly facing the lagoons, were mostly made of *ravenale* with a thatched roof that offered an absolutely unique atmosphere which encouraged deep communion with nature. No electricity, only kerosene lamps, that needed daily maintenance in order to be re-utilized every evening.

These days of relaxation, spent in a healthy and happy atmosphere, were quite exceptional.

As all his cousins and friends were of French origin, they shared the same culture, the same faith, and the same sense of humour that constantly animated their conversations. This jovial atmosphere enwrapped them, wherever they passed, wherever their adventures led them. From fishing to horse-racing, from soirees around game tables to trips on foot or by car.

Since the organization of the first World Cups, football imposed itself more and more as an international sport. The cousins were elated by a round ball, often devising some new rules that were particular to their group.

Hyacinth was happy when immersed in these varried atmospheres, where friendship was pure and profound, nourished by captivating activities and fascinating conversations.

However he did not always manage to express himself on what he really felt, or to share those deep questions that sometimes perturbed him. He often needed to be left alone just to be silent and to meditate, in order to find his inner self, to seek answers to his questions, to pursue his quest.

Sometimes, when he closed his eyes, two lights shone in the bottom of his heart and he did not know to which one of these lights he had to expose himself to in order to advance further on . He had fallen in love with Eda, his cousin with whom he had shared games when he was still a little boy. They loved each other, this first spark having been fed by their growing love.

This emotion had surprised him one day, while they were in the orchard of Labourdonnais. The group of cousins were walking towards the house after having eaten mangoes to their full. The two of them found themselves at the end of the file walking slowly, chatting. Although they felt the desire to be on their own, rather than joining the group, their reason dictated them to follow the others. Walking side by side, at turtle pace, as if to stretch the time of this exquisite motherent, and once bending in front of a mango tree to pick up some fruits, their cheeks brushed against each other. That day, Hyacinthe was overwhelmed by a trembling, like a discharge that had warmed up his blood and dilated his heart. He knew he was blushing, but had said nothing. Neither did she. They had simply looked at each other and smiled.

He cherished the memory of this motherent under the mango tree when Eda's smile had ravished him, while the birds, in a concert of songs, chirping and serenading, invaded the orchard in search of a shelter, before nightfall. The sparks of the setting sun projected oblique rays that ignited the surrounding trees with orange and gold tints. In this fairy-like atmosphere, their love had revealed itself.

Later, with beating hearts, they had been able to put words to their feelings, to declare their flame, to assert their urge to see each other again. This relationship warmed up their otherwise well balanced and fulfilling lives.

Their favourite meeting place was Sans Souci, that domain of the Rovillard family, farther than Cap Malheureux. Hyacinthe had been there a few times when he was a child. Then, during his adolescence, being invited by his cousin Yves, he had visited more and more often, immersing himself in the cheerful and affectionate swing of cousins!

Eda was always present, discreet, never leaving the sight of him, listening with attention, to the eldest's conversation. But since the motherent of that smile under the mango-tree in the orchard of Labourdonnais, Hyacinthe had understood that the visits to his cousin Yves were in reality a pretext to see Eda. He secretely understood that it was mainly her presence that attracted him to this family place, where they could spend time together between card games and seaside strolls.

A sweet certainty persuaded him that she was the unique pearl that could fulfill his entire life. They finally got engaged on 17 April 1941. He was 24 years old, she had just celebrated her 21st birthday on 12 April. This engagement day marked him profoundly. Two years later, in the middle of the desert, he wrote in one of his notebooks:

Yesterday, two years ago, I celebrated my official engagement. How prevent a certain nostalgia - I should say: a great nostalgia - to take hold of me on such an occasion? Then, it was happiness; today it is only a memory! But isn't it already a consolation that the memory is still there?

Just a few days ago, the expanse of the desert on the route border was dazzling with green plants and with flowers, but today the first sand storms have had their effect. All this green is grilled, dusty, disgusting; the flowers have all gone except a few thistles that still resist.

In 1940, although engaged to Eda, Hyacinthe was however not serene. He felt torn deep down because the other light hidden in his soul kept on shining: small, sure, but whose intense brightness beckoned him all the time. It could not be clearly defined. It was a fire that sparkled a yearning for something else, for something bigger still than the love of a spouse. It was characterised by a growing desire, a secret attraction, for an ideal that could not realise itself in a comfortable and conventional family life. It was as if this fire urgently needed to surrender itself without holding back, with no return, with no half measures.

At times, he happend to sit down at the seaside, for long moments, in the shadow of filao trees, resting his soul while scrutinizing the horizon line. The clouds that moved in the distance made him dream. He imagined himself in an airplane, plunged in the infinity of the sky, flying at ocean level to the distant continents.

He had preciously preserved the book '*Terre des Hommes*' by St. Exupéry, which was first published at the end of 1939. The reading of this book had produced in him a disturbing effect. This little fire that was secretly shining had been fed by this narrative of great a adventure amidst sky and desert.

The discovery of these pages, in which the author relates the extreme situations that he had experienced, had opened in him new vast horizons, and in one night only, his choices that had seemed so evident to him before, were put back into question. He kept moving ahead, though, whilst his inward lights revealed themselves more and more clearly in his heart and in his thoughts.

The effects of the world conflicts were already being felt in Mauritius. On September 1939, the world was at war again, and Hyacinthe sought to understand the reasons and stakes of that situation.

The Mauritian population felt more intensively the anguish of war, and even apprehended an invasion of the island. For this reason, Monsignor Leen, Bishop of Port-Louis, decided to build on the flank of Signal Mountain which dominated the port and the capital, a sanctuary dedicated to Mary, Queen of Peace. The project was entrusted to the architects Boullé-Lagesse, and Hyacinthe was of course associated with the conception of this monument.

At the beginning of May 1940, the first stone was laid and soon grown-ups and young ones went there to pray to Our Lady asking her to protect the island and to grant it the gift of peace. The site was inaugurated three years later and remained an emblematic site on the island.

It became the theatre of large assemblies such as the Mass celebrated by Saint John Paul II on 14 October 1989, or even more, the funerals of Cardinal Jean Margéot, on 19 July 2009.

While pursuing his Mauritian lifestyle, Hyacinth resisted, with more and more difficulty, the call that devoured him. How to keep a deaf ear to that little voice that murmured: «*And you? Why don't you go to defend the Nation?*»

He was fighting this desire to enlist , as he was deeply conscious that both his mother and his fiancée needed him. What should he do? Leave or stay? He weighted the pros and cons, evaluated the advantages and disadvantages, measured the risks... To leave or to stay? This was a crucial question that haunted him, a decisive question that prevented him from sleeping. What for? Who for?

The succession of questions drew him to the depth of his soul into the sanctuary where one asks oneself about the meaning of life, a sanctuary where no-one can penetrate, and where there is no one else but oneself to face choices, to face decisions that will decide for one's existence.

Many Mauritians had enlisted in the First World War. Certainly, in proportion to the population, the number of soldiers leaving the Indian Ocean colony remained weak, but it was sufficient for Mauritius to be represented in this big war. And like each country, each town or village, Mauritius had also lost its children in 1914-1918.

Many families, including the Rouillard family, had been affected by these tragedies. An elder cousin of Antoinette, Amédée Rouillard, had died in Mesopotamia, the actual Iraq!

A monument erected in their memory, in front of the Royal College of Curepipe, proclaimed the unanimous wish that this tragedy would never happen again.

But this was denied a little more than twenty years later!

Another atrocious war was again ravaging the old continent, and the entire world. And as for the first world war, a maximum of human energy and brainpower were needed to serve as counter force to the enemy. The highest possible number of men had to be transformed into offensive and defensive machines. Propaganda spread into the colonies, to the farthest countries, to the forgotten islands at the end of the world.

To appeal to Mauritian patriotism all offices and public buildings exhibited photos of King George VI, of the royal family, of the emblematic Prime Ministers, Sir Winston Churchill, and even of Marshall Montgomery.

When the remarkable cruiser *Mauritius* transited in Port-Louis with 920 enrolled marines, many Mauritians felt like crossing the Rubicon.

Later, Mauritius was going to offer to the English Airforce two *Spitfires*, one hydroplane for that cruiser, as well as several mobile canteens to the city of London. These donations were possible thanks to a public subscription, and to funds resulting from special horseracing competitions organized on 26 October 1942 by the Mauritius Turf Club and the Mauritius Jockey Club.

But more than donations in nature, Mauritius offered many of its children to the British army to battle alongside the Allies.

From July 1940, several Mauritians joined *Special Operations Executive* (SOE) which was just created. They had to act as secret agents in several regions, sustain the network of Resistance in countries occupied by the Germans. The Mauritians were especially appreciated for their bilingualism. On the island a few streets bear the names of war heroes like Maurice Larcher, Odette Ernest. etc.

In 1940, the first effect of war was a decrease in communications. Foreign ships were rare in the harbour of Port-Louis. All commercial activities were slowed down.

The company "Messageries Maritimes" no longer docked, and, consequently, supplies diminished and food had to be rationed . Each citizen was weekly allocated five pounds of rice, three pounds of flour, tow pounds of dry grains, two pounds of sugar, three pounds of corn or four pounds of potatoes.

The government forced the sugar industry to allot twenty percent of its land to food cultivation, such as corn, manioc and potato, in order to answer the population's needs.

The island became vulnerable despite its distance from the world conflicts. Sirens were installed, refuges built, schools requisitioned for military use. Mail was henceforth submitted to censure.

Another source of worry during the war: the diseases affecting the population, for instance malaria or tuberculosis.

Without doubt, under the influence of this increasingly difficult atmosphere, Hyacinthe tackled the hard question that was constantly haunting him and decided to leave. No one pressed him. On the contrary, he had many reasons for staying home: to take care of his widowed mother, to marry his fiancée whom he loved immensely , to contribute to the island's development ...

But it was stronger than him. Of course, it would have been easier to stay or to postpone his decision. But in the secret of his soul, in the intimacy of his conscience, he was ready.

One thing was to take a decision, another thing was to share that decision. Would those close to him understand? How would they react?

He opted to speak to his mother Antoinette first. He trusted her to understand his choice. One day, whilst they were on their own at Labourdonnais, he seized this opportunity to open his heart to her. She had listened to him without interrupting. With her great sensitivity and maternal intuition, she had already anticipated that such a decision was maturing in her son's heart, But with respect and patience, she had prayed for him as usual and had waited for him to speak to her about it.

She found the appropriate words to support him in this noble and courageous entreprise. In the family, there were already a few examples of cousins or friends who had made the same choice, and Antoinette had had the time to meditate on what the young men would be feeling in regard to this call for enlistment.

After his mother's benediction, Hyacinthe felt still stronger in his decision It was harder however to announce it to Eda. She visited on the same day at Labourdonnais and he had to find the adequate words, the appropriate tone of voice, the way of speaking that would justify his choice without being too rough on her. As this was not easy, he had suggested to her to take a walk in the orchard in search of some fruits.

They entered the small lane that led from the house. The dog followed them. Watching them from the window with deep feelings, Antoinette turned towards Heaven and begged: «*Oh God! Take care of your children!*»

The young *fiancés* were holding hands. The dog ran ahead of them and came back towards them, while searching for something in the thickets. They disappeared behind the tall centenarian trees.

This motherent was painful for both. The prospect of departure broke their hearts. Eda too had had quite a premonition that such a decision could arise at any time, as they had often talked about the war and about those who were leaving to join the troops in Europe or North Africa. She had already sensed that something was occuring in Hyacinth's heart: mysterious motions out of her reach, deep aspirations way beyond her. Once the decision taken, the future was losing its brightness. How could one try not to imagine the worst despite all comforting words and precautions taken by Hyacinthe to minimize the risks involved?

She had ended up crying, and he had found it hard to bear those tears that tore his heart down. They were approaching the mango-tree where their eyes had met for the first time, where their smiles had then brightened the orchard at the end of the day. They hugged each other and, in silence, their tears interwined.

Without really measuring the weight of his words, but in order to console her, he looked at her and made this promise: «*I will come back*». These words echoed in her and did her the greatest good, because they were both convincing and soft. She could not help crying however. With his finger, he traced their initials on the mango-tree, as if to sign a deal.

Eventually, the whole family learnt the news and the anxieties of the ones or the others were softened by the pride they felt concerning Hyacinthe and his enlistment, his determination, his abnegation.

A few weeks later, he left the architecture office to enter a new phase of his life that started with a period of training at Vacoas, at the headquarters of the Special Mobile Force, now in full ebullition. Luckily, he could not guess about the consequences of his enlistment. This is true of any commitment that claims a total self-denial.

This first motherentum of generosity would doubtless have never been possible without a certain under-estimation of both the hard realities that laid beyond, and of the difficult times ahead.

While, together with several fellows, he was preparing to leave his native land, elsewhere a huge migration was already dragging entire families away from their homelands. Masses of people were starting to flee danger at the peril of their lives.

Thus, at the end of 1940, Mauritius welcomed a contingency of Jews, fugitives from Central Europe, who had not been able to enter Palestine. Deported by Great Britain, 1,500 men, women and children arrived in Mauritius on 9 December 1940.

These Jews left the Mauritian soil at the end of the war, on 25 August 1945, and the majority of them made their way towards Palestine.

Of the initial group, 126 died in Mauritius during the war and were buried in an enclave of Saint Martin Cemetery, in the western part of the island.

The Jewish people were living a crucial motherent of their history. The world did not know it yet, but the *Shoah* had started and it would lead to the creation of the State of Israel in 1948.

Hyacinthe would have the opportunity to set foot on the Promised Land, to travel through a large number of countries and to get acquainted with quite different people. But at the end of 1940, he was quite satisfied to stay with his own people in the heart of the austral Summer.

They celebrated Christmas with the family. As happened every year, he joined his brothers and sisters, his sisters-in-law, his brother-in-law, his nephews and nieces, to gather round Antoinette, who was so happy to bring together her children and grandchildren in the joy of the Nativity.

Before taking to the sea he enjoyed these precious moments to the full.

The rest of the story is directly told to us by Hyacinthe himself throughout his notebooks. On the 8, then the 12 March 1941, in the Geneifa Camp, he starts reporting from his departure from Mauritius and shares the feelings that had swept through him during the pressing moments of his exile.

The grand Departure

Those lines that I start today are only some notes scribbled haphazardly by my pen at leisure times, some personal impressions on my life as a soldier - I do not wish to call it a journal. My purpose in writing them is to be able to go over them one day, in better times, and to revive the memories which otherwise would perhaps fade from my mind.

What memories? I am afraid they do not seem to be the best of my life. But isn't it often a way to appreciate even more the present motherent when one remembers past sufferings?

If I am not allowed to return to my own, I wish that these writings be sent to the persons whom I love most in the world, to my mother and my *fiancée*. I wish, if God accepts the sacrifice of my life that I am now offering to Him, that these lines be for them the last testimony of a love that I have perhaps never been able to express to them.

Since the beginning of war, I have wished to fulfill my duty towards my country by enrolling myself in one of the Imperial Forces.

My candidature for enrolment in aviation not being accepted, I thought, when the Mauritius Artisan Works Organization was founded, that it was where I would serve to the best of my capacities.

So am I officer of the Engineering Forces since 7 January,! Should I speak of the sacrifice that such an action represents for me? Leaving behind those one loves, exile oneself, risk one's life, abandon one's comfort and the pleasant things which existence has to offer us, can one understand what this means when one hasn't endured such an experience oneself?

First and above all, leaving those one loves, *that is* the real sacrifice for me, the type of suffering which can be measured to the full only through experience. "*Man is an apprentice, pain is his master, and no-one really knows himself as long as he has not suffered*", said Musset. May I know myself better and above all improve myself.

I have started these notes a little late to be able to narrate in detail my journey from Mauritius to here. And besides, didn't I say before that this is not a journal that I write? I shall only try therefore, just to put down a few memories.

16 January has become for me one of the dates that one can never forget: it marks the beginning of a new phase in my life, and will remain engraved in my memory as quite a painful day.

"To leave is to die a little!" How right was the poet in writing these words! When I kissed Mother and Eda for the last time before leaving, I understood the heartbreak of such a separation. Quite soon after this *adieu*, I left the house, without even turning back, without a last waiving of my hand, I perhaps almost ran as fast as I could, from those whom I was leaving.

Was it cowardice on my part? It's hard for me to say, I only felt that I would not have enough courage.

And at Port-Louis again, before embarking, I ask myself now if it would not have been better that I had not said *'Good bye'* to anyone. I feel that I would not have been able to refrain myself, or hid my emotions that were already overflowing out of my heart. I can see it again and I'll never forget: Eda, my brothers, my friends, running on the quay in order to see me one last time. Eda, in her blue dress, gesturing to me with her hand, and disappearing from my view as the tugboat pulled away gradually.

A little while later, I was on the *Talamba*. Once my luggage down in my cabin, I tried to get acquainted with the ship, at least to get enough information in order to find my way in the curves of its stairways. This was quite rapidly carried out in the *Talamba*, which, in spite of its three chimneys and its majestic appearance, is not a big ship. It is not luxurious but comfortable enough - especially for the first class passengers. How I would appreciate now the comforts I had on board!

I shall leave the ship aside now to talk about the First Class passengers, that is, the group of officers that we were. Besides the major Taylor, and Baker-Cromwell, both in my company, there were six officers, Georges Mayer, Philippe Guimbeau and Roland Duclos of 'No 1 Coy' and Hervé Brown, Georges Leclos, and Jean Baissac of *'No 2 Coy'*. I already knew my mates quite well, or most of them. The atmosphere augured quite favourably for the journey.

We only left Mauritius on the 17 January around seven o'clock, as our escort, an Australian auxiliary Cruiser, arrived only at that motherent. The four days of voyage between Mauritius and Durban have been quite unpleasant: the sea was rough, the first days particularly, and most of us, if not actually sick, were not better off.

The 21st in the morning, we arrived at Durban, and accosted one of the quays in the afternoon. As I had travelled at too young an age to remember, I shall not exaggerate by saying that my first impression of this big city with its pretty buildings and its lights, was one of sheer marvel. The difference between Mauritius and that country was too big. I found no point of comparison. At the end of a few days however, I could assess everything objectively and criticize whatever deserved to be.

Unfortunately, just as for most big buildings, the too fertile imagination of the architects, in desperate need of decors, disfigures works that promised to be otherwise lovely. I saw here and there a few facades of Dutch style - grand gables whose straight lines are interrupted here and there by circular arches surrounded by mouldings, windows with lintels decorated with *arabesque* and doors of a particular form. I did not like that style too much, and I find that, like all styles of a past age, it can be adapted and modified to new needs.

I stop now this dissertation where I have been side-tracked, more by my passion for architectural art than by any claim to knowledge.

After departing from Durban on the 29th, we only arrived at Suez, or rather Port Tewfik, on the 16th February, after 18 days of travel between sky and water.

I think that if we were satisfied with the companionship of our 'Chief Engineer', it has been reciprocal. On the day before our arrival, he told us that we were certainly the most well-behaved among all the troops having journeyed on the *Talamba,* and he was too outspoken to have been lying. I appreciated the fact that Mauritians received such a compliment from an Englishman.

On the morning of the 17th, the first ones embarked at 8 am by train for a camp near the Pyramids, where they must still be now. Our company only left by foot at 9,30 am, for our camp at Geneifa, a distance of about 35 miles.

12 March 1941

As I set foot at Port Tewfik, I understood that here everything is directed towards the same goal: the war, or rather the victory. If at Durban, I had been impressed by the amount of soldiers in the streets, by the number of military vehicles that were being embarked for the Middle East or by the quantity of troop transports, it was not less true that civil life had still the larger place. Here, nothing of all that: anti-air batteries, campaign canons, trains loaded with war materials, and everywhere, uniforms, nothing but uniforms - that was what I saw around me and that continues to form part of the environment in which I live.

As I said previously, we embarked around 9.30 am in a convoy of trucks that had come to take us, and we left towards our destination.

This voyage was for me the first contact with, I should not say the desert, as it is not exactly that, but: the sand of Egypt. Little by little, the sandy plain was beginning to appear until it formed the only horizon. We advanced this way up to Fayed where we were told our camp was.

Geneifa is situated on the road from Ismailia to Suez, exactly to the South of Great Bitter Lake. From the South-West to the South-East, stands a chain of mountains, or rather of sandy little hills; the Bitter Lake stretches from North-West to North East, bordered by date trees on our shore, while the Sinai Desert forms the opposite side, and the rest of the horizon is but a lowland where we are.

The larger part of Geneifa Camp is composed of tents, the number of which varies according to the importance of each unit. I would not be able to mention with precision the total length, but I think I don't exaggerate by estimating it at 6 miles, starting from the aviators, who are the first in line to the last 'cage' of Italian prisoners of war.

It won't take too much time to describe our sector. A certain professional deformation has inspired me to draw a little schematic plan which could only be understood with a certain amount of good will. But isn't it Napoleon who said that " *Sometimes a small sketch is worth more than a long report*"?

When we had disembarked and when I realized that it was there that we would live henceforth, I confess that I was shocked. I had entertained no illusion as to what awaited me, it is true, but neither did I ever have experienced anything of what I found in reality.

That yellowish dust mixed to the pebbles, which forms the soil of the camp as well as the floor of our tents, the tents themselves where nothing had been installed yet, the feeling of isolation that all of a sudden appeared to me in all its reality, all that confused me for a motherent. I have unfortunately such a character that generally matters of no great importance make me unhappy.

Our first day in camp consisted in particular of organizing the tents: dresser, mess or store, and in planning the meals for the men.

This question of meals has been one of the big difficulties during approximately the first two weeks of our stay here. The list of food items that were to constitute the ration had been devised in Mauritius by the Health Department. This list, which was just good enough for Mauritius, both quality wise and quantity wise, became a true headache in Egypt where certain items, such as rice, are very difficult to obtain... In addition, the quantity was utterly insufficient, especially compared to what the other troops, Europeans or Indians, and even the war prisoners, received.

Thanks to the complaints and efforts of Major Taylor, this situation has now changed. A report has besides been addressed to the Mauritian authorities on this subject, expressing the troops' dissatisfaction and the difficulties and complications that could result. An anonymous letter addressed by one of the members of the Company to the Commandment in Chief of Forces in the Middle East complaining of this treatment, has even been intercepted on time - this was the mindset that started to prevail.

As I already said, a new scale of rationing has now been established and the men are delighted with what they receive.

I am unfortunately a bad observer, and not a fine psychologist; the impressions that I shall note, if they are not completely false, will perhaps be imperfect. I only knew Duncan Taylor by sight before starting my training course in Vacoas last December. I knew also, from those who knew him well, that he was a good worker, a straight man and 'bon bougre' (good chap), which summarizes everything. Besides, the fact that a man of his age, with a wife and children, in a well-off position and who has apparently everything needed to be happy, and on top of it all, having participated in the last war, volunteered his services for his country, is an attitude before which everyone should bow down, a stand that can only be expected from someone with high moral values.

Major Taylor always knows what he wants and how to obtain it too, although without any abruptness. In the mess, he is a most pleasant companion: he adds to some technical knowledge a lively intelligence which, without being studied, is of the most interesting sort. Always ready to laugh and not deprived of humour, he contributes to a large extent to giving us a cheerfulness without which I prefer not to imagine what would be our life - on me personally, his good humour has a considerable influence.

In addition, we both come from Mauritius - we can talk about what we left behind - often he talks to me about Eda and her family, whom he knows a little - and I forget that I am in exile.

In the end I would say that if I had the choice for a 'Company Commander', it would certainly be Duncan Taylor whom I would choose.

I now come to the captain Baker-Crosswell or B.C. as we call him. What strikes is, that as a person he is short of flexibility, could we say, with feelings so rigid that they seem to be also under military discipline. His determination, his will, his zeal at work, and I believe I can say, his courage, denote a strong character that is softened by nothing. He sticks to discipline in a very strict manner, and expects the same from everyone else; his orders have to be obeyed to the letter and he sees to it that they are; he puts a lot of himself in his work and does so more than he is supposed to, but he admits of no inertia on the part of anyone.

17 March 1941: It has been a month since we settled here. Even if it may seem paradoxical to me, first of all I have to say that these first weeks have seemed to pass very fast; to be constantly occupied, to look for an occupation, if necessary not to let inactivity bring up thoughts that cannot breed anything but discouragement, that is how I trained my will till now, and I am happy of the result achieved.

I have not yet described two places where I spend a certain part of my day: my tent and the 'officers' mess'. My tent especially deserves that I stop for a morerent on its subject. A cone of cloth whose base measures about 12 feet in diameter, surrounded by a heap of sand about 2 feet high: that is the exterior appearance of my dwelling place. One enters it, or rather descends into it - for the rules of passive defence seem to doom us to burial, alive or dead - by an opening made on one side.

The first night I only opened my bed and threw my suitcases in a corner, on the sand; my tent diffused utter desolation, and truly I was discouraged.

The next day, I started to get it organised: I watered and flattened the soil - as the sand contained a rather high proportion of clay, a quite hard surface can thus be obtained - then spread out the bags to be used as carpets. This done, I found two containers of gasoline and a board, that I transformed into a toilet table: after that it was a case of condensed milk and a case of 'corned beef' which, each covered with a towel, can be used, till now, as a table and a cabinet.

The latest newcomer among my furniture is a luxury item: it is a small table of white wood that one of the sergeants had had made by one of our carpenters, and which looks really great.

I forgot to mention my camp armchair which, after having assembled its parts with quite difficulty, I use more to spread out my clothes than as a chair. It is very useful to me.

As a result of all this, I am now very comfortable in my new dwelling. How far I am, however, from the comfort of my room in Mauritius! Yes, all this is quite far, but I don't complain, I am satisfied with my life right now, I am happy to serve my country by accepting these privations - and I am happy to endure this ordeal which, by granting me a new experience of life, will earn me the right to be called a man.

To come back to my tent, I said that I was confortable there. What I particularly appreciate is that it is a place where I am at home, where no one enters without asking for my permission; the setting of the furniture and items, a photo of Mother and one of Eda on my table have gifted it with a certain personality, have made it a place where I can retire and be myself again. It is here that I come to write these notes, on my own with my thoughts, it is here that I am able to dream about those I love.

I said that I would now speak about the 'officers' mess'. It is a big tent which, like mine, was not attractive at all at our arrival. But here too, with patience and a little ingenuousness, we have come to install ourselves adequately.

A separate section in the corner serves as a pantry; the rest of the tent is our 'living-room'; the floor is covered with linoleum and a carpet, three military tables, four wicker armchairs and, since a few days ago, two armchairs and a game of darts, have transformed it into a place where we get together with pleasure after work.

The 18 March, we were visited by quite a character: Major General Hughes, Engineer in Chief, Middle East, accompanied by an officer of his Army Staff, the Lieutenant-Colonel Saint George.

I believe that we shall have more work, or at least more interesting work. Moreover, it is perhaps owing to his visit that I was affected to the detachment in which I am presently, and that the company is leaving Geneifa, as I have heard the day before yesterday, for a destination of which I have no idea. I have been annoyed, however, to hear that our work would consist only in building constructions in Egypt itself.

I don't wish to spend the duration of war at the rear, without witnessing to danger, without even hearing the cannon. It's true that everyone has a definite task, and that those who work at the base, just like the soldiers of the front, contribute to victory.

However, I need so much to 'feel' the war up close, to run risks, that spending time in the rear would never offer me!

If it is not permitted for me to be on the front during the battle itself, I would like at least to be as close as possible to it, to be in places which have been operational theatres. A certain spirit of adventure is urging me to want to leave the frontiers of Egypt, to 'see the country'. I console myself with the thought that maybe this will happen; my fate will depend on the way things will turn out.

I had a conversation of a few minutes with the Lieutenant-Colonel Saint George, who accompanied the General. Like many others, he was astonished to learn that I was born in Mauritius and that I had never left the country.

I have not yet talked about my occupations at Geneifa, I mean the construction work where I was involved. In fact it is so unimportant that I could let it easily pass by in silence.

Between Bitter Lake and our camp, about one mile distant from the latter, there is a R.E. Dump - that is a warehouse of materials under the control of the Engineering department. It is at this warehouse that I worked before my arrival here. We were assigned the construction of 'Nissen huts', a job that very soon becomes very tiring by its simplicity. The 'Nissen hut' is a construction made of removable components ; it consists of a series of solid semi-circular metal structures linked by wooden spans, the roof is made of undulated corrugated iron, and the inside is panelled by sheets of isolation material. The doors and windows are adjusted between the trusses on the lateral surfaces, and the extremities of the building end with a brick wall or a plank partition.

We had to assemble five of these constructions and then build a concrete floor. They were to serve as stores for certain materials. I should say here that the quantity of materials that this warehouse can contain - which is nevertheless ironically called a 'small dump'- is really impressive. From the rolls of barbed wired which rise up to a mount of 20 feet high, to the corrugated iron sheets and iron bars, all numbered here by tens of thousands, to the bath tubs and wash basins, probably for hospital use, of which I counted several hundreds. I said that my work was rather boring; Nevertheless, I appreciate having acquired a knowhow that I did not have in Mauritius.

At the Mauritius Building, or at Hall Geneve Langlois, it was almost exclusively office work that I had to do: my occasional visits to the construction sites did not allow me to follow a building operation close enough. Here, I was closely involved with the execution of a job and with the team organization. I thus had the opportunity to see the way in which work is done in the army. I noted certain practical work methods, but did not always agree with sergeants on the means of implementation. I could also assess for myself that the waste reputation in the army is not a legend.

The management of carpenters' and masons' teams was, as I said, my main occupation. At the same time, the routine was quite simple and I had nothing much to do: at the beginning of our arrival, we had a parade of physical exercise and of instruction from caporals at 6,30 am every morning. After some time, this first parade was fortunately abolished, and the time of assembly for the work was changed from 8 am to 7 am.

As soon as we were settled at the camp, the major entrusted me with a task which, without being too complicated, is none of those that I would have chosen with pleasure; What I mean is my liability as 'mess-secretary'.

I have always felt a certain indifference, I would even say quite a clear aversion, for everything that concerns housekeeping and the kitchen. It is useless to add that my ignorance in this area is, to say the least, vast. I don't think that I would be able to fry an egg - in any case I have never tried - and the elaboration of a menu has never been an art in which I have excelled.

And so, from one day to the next, I became the 'housekeeper' and, perhaps a more distressing problem, I also had to do bookkeeping! It is true that regarding three persons, the accounts for the kitchen, for the bar, and for the housekeeping in general are not that complicated.

Accounting has always been a nightmare for me. I have always done my accounting in my own way, which is certainly not very orthodox; I had now to do my bookkeeping according to all the principles of the art, so that it could be audited at any time.

Slowly however, I have adapted myself to my new role: to check the rations, watch over the quantity of eggs used every day, make sure that the kitchen towels are not shabby, and vary - with sometimes very limited means - the monotony of meals, became for me a habit. Besides, I often received the major's congratulations or those of B.C., especially about the way of 'disguising' things as indigestible as the 'meat loaf'.

I had never enjoyed such a good appetite as I have since my arrival in Egypt to the extent that my brand new uniforms are already tight on me.

Hyacinthe was a contemplative and he spent time to rest his sight, his heart and thoughts, by admiring the beauty of nature that surrounded him. Even in the desert, he found enough stock to feed his meditation, but he was always drawn back to the reality of a war in which he was now involved.

There are also flowers in the desert! I mean, real flowers, little delicate corollas swaying at the top of their stem, surrounded by green leaves, as fragrant as their sisters in the fields or gardens. Flowers with sweet and varied hues, whose colors harmonize and complete each other, flowers of which no gardener has assembled the various shades, but which are there to prove the existence of the Master by their very presence, if not by their delicacy. It is in the sand dunes that I have seen them today, these little flowers.

Sand dunes whose white color is almost too harsh for the too clear sky. There are a few date-trees all dishevelled, which hug and jostle each other: green and dark stains adding freshness to this sand's white glare.

And at the foot of the date-trees, here are the flowers! First of all it is a green tapestry. Since the small flowers have realized that before anything else what is needed is to mitigate this burning white of the sand, they addressed their plants' green leaves for that purpose. They need those green leaves as a casket. They are delicate, they would burn from the too-white sand's exposure.

A large tapestry of green leaves that unrolls itself and now turns into a golden napkin, an ocean of little yellow heads all proud to show their brilliance. And each has its own face, these yellow heads: gold buttons, bells, marigolds.

Some are all pale, others orange. A beautiful color, all warm. Others are bright yellow, of this yellow which is tiring if not alternated with a little bit of purple. And here it is, the purple, and also some blue. Here, fine braids of a light blue, which the wind sways softly, there lavender or violet little bells, farther away, at ground level, a profusion of tiny flowers, of a beautiful ocean-blue, petals all open to the sun.

The symphony in blue and yellow extends in its green frame. A scale of tones that complete each other and harmonize, but where a high note is missing. But no! Here it is, that note, which hinders the threatening monotony: some red poppies. Oh! not a lot of poppies! Only one or two tufts thrown here and there. They don't need to be numerous, these little red poppies! They are of such a beautiful color, so shiny! Who would dare not to see them!

And at the foot of the sand dunes, the flower-beds extend according to their sinuosities, sometimes widening, sometimes all narrow.

But what is this here?

A barricade of barbed wires to which are hung, here and there, some writing boards with skulls and bones!

A minefield?

Yes, Indeed, I have to admit to myself: all my pretty flowers, my blue and gold tapestry, do nothing but cover up devices where death lies in waiting for those who venture there.

Let us go back now: the dream was too beautiful!

Crossing The Desert

Hyacinthe had immersed himself quite easily into this new universe of war. Memories of Mauritius remained still alive in him and helped him to accept his new life. New bonds of friendship were made, in particular with the major Taylor who comforted him greatly.

He managed to acquire some self-control so as to be able to bear all those hardships that were not lacking. In this desert, so many things drew him away from the Mauritian context! His strength and his generosity were however to be put to test to the point of drying up his heart which had maintained so far the warmth of Mauritius and of those dear to him.

The morning of 14 March, there was a quite unpleasant breeze, not strong enough however to prevent the parade from taking place at 8 a.m.

As usual, each team was assigned to its customary task: I went off after some time to supervise the work of masons of the 'R.E.Dump'. As the men worked inside the building, it took me some time to realize the violence of the wind that increased from hour to hour: when I went out, the storm was hitting full force; the sand was lifted up by real clouds and created an almost compact atmosphere. I told the sergeant to come back immediately to camp with the men - a distance of about a mile - and I went off on my own.

It was not going to be an easy task to accomplish that journey: I could hardly move forward, having to walk against the wind, the sand entered my eyes, nose and mouth, and visibility was such that at some moments I lost my way, not seeing further than 30 feet ahead.

Back in my tent, it was a spectacle of desolation that I discovered: the sand had started to cover everything; my toilet table, bed, shoes were full of it; some objects still remaining on the floor were half buried; and, what appeared to me a bigger danger, my tent seemed to be unable to resist any longer from the violence of the wind.

In a few instants, I had packed everything in my suitcase and rolled up my covers, ready now to face the disaster of my roof collapsing, and I went out to consolidate the other tents and take the necessary measures.

Towards noon, the storm had reached its utmost intensity: I had to remain outside a long time to knock down a few tents that could not hold - we lost two of them which ripped completely - and reinforce the ropes of the others.

During those few hours, the sand grains hit my face, arms and legs with such a force that, at certain moments, I had to stop working and seek protection somewhere else.

In spite of the motorcyclist's special glasses that the headquarters had lent me, I had to stop once in a while to remove a huge layer of sand from my eyes.

Useless to say that, for lunch, sand constituted the main ingredient of all the dishes: the slightest boiled vegetable was rendered crunchy to taste!

Our appetite was nevertheless good enough to make us appreciate the dish.

The storm lasted the whole day - a day that seemed terribly long to me. For the first time since my arrival, I felt really discouraged.

Who has not once been overcome by a nondescript feeling before the outbursts of the elements? The forces of nature, more than anything else make us acknowledge the vast degree of our powerlessness, as well as that of our weakness. No fear, no anguish, but a great melancholy: that was the feeling that fell on me, which I was not strong enough to resist. A thought overwhelmed me completely: my isolation, my separation from my country and from all those I love.

In the afternoon, with the end of the storm, the wind had decreased in intensity. I saw my dark thoughts vanish and the major's good spirits quickly helped me to recover completely.

The account of the sand storm is a beautiful illustration of the interior struggles as well as the inner storm that Hyacinthe would be confronted with. As often in the life of a human being, after the enthusiasms of the beginning, and the burst of generosity that urges to a commitment, come the more sober moments.

The interior storms were going to intensify with more and more violence: owing to all disillusions, disappointments and an array of difficulties just too hard to bear.

He drew some comfort when he found a few oases in those secret deserts: during a leave, or by way of a swim in the sea or, still more, of a mail received. However, those times of rest and resourcing were a double-edged sword as they provided a good feeling on the spur of the motherent, but could gradually nurture a nostalgia of the past, a melancholy, or even anxieties about the future. And here was the big difficulty: to accept the present motherent without travelling into what might have been one's life in the past, nor in what could happen in the future.

The first strong sensations were the bombardments on the day of his arrival, which Hyacinthe described in his first note-book:

On the very day of our arrival, we had our first air-raid alert: in the middle of the day, I had to spend half an hour in a slit-tunnel with the other officers, waiting for airplanes that we never saw or heard.

At night, towards midnight, the alarm went off a second time. I did not need to get out of my bed, the sand par-jets forming a sufficient protection around my tent. This time detonations of anti-aerial cannons and bombs could be heard: the explosion of one bomb of large calibre was even loud enough to make us feel the commotion. Although the bombardment occurred far enough from here, in the direction of Suez, I learnt afterward that there was no damage done that night.

If that raid was fruitless, it has to be said that some time before the Italians or the Germans had had some successes in their attacks against the Canal.

By means of parachuted mines, they sank three or four ships and succeeded in stopping the traffic for a while. One has to acknowledge that the enemy planes that come up here are doing a pretty job. Their closest base is Rhodes, and the distance there and return represents about 200 miles.

One understands in his writings that there was not only the violence of impact when the explosion of the bombs was heard, but also the tension of waiting, the intuition of the threat, and the difficult check of one's imagination. It is in this manner that false alerts could tax on the nerves.

On 3 April, there was a motherent of anguish:

Towards midnight, I was awoken by the sound of voices near the major's tent, and as I lent an ear, I heard the word 'big' popping up several times in the conversation. I went immediately to see what was happening and met the captain (...) who thought that we were being gassed .

There was in the atmosphere a special smell, somewhat reminiscent of rubber, and what could be vapours of mustard gas.

What should we do in such a situation? We did not yet have our masks - which, by the way, have not yet been delivered till now - and nothing to replace them. My first feeling was a fear that panic would prevail among the men (...)

After a while, though, I realized that the smell that floated in the air was the same as the one I had smelt in Suez, which came from the oil refinery; I also thought of the impossibility of an attack on such a large objective as Geneifa, so far from any Italian base; one last reassuring factor was the wind, fast enough to purify the atmosphere if ever it was poisoned.

That night, Hyacinthe decided to go to bed... He finally understood that nothing serious had happened.

Often, rumours were also sources of worry. Not the announcement of an imminent attack but news more or less founded from the front. These announcements were more and more frequent and sometimes alarming.

Hyacinthe had the opportunity to visit Cairo quite often, either on punctual supply missions, or for several days of leave. As a good tourist, he was attentive to the smallest details, and always with a special attention to the buildings' architecture. And like any good tourist, he was cheated by the merchants who charged him high prices.

All these memories of Cairo were systematically noted:

The first impression that I felt was not extraordinary. A lot of streets are narrow, with very ordinary stores or boutiques, the tramways and buses are ancient devices and there is no local flavour.

However, what I found quite picturesque, were the carts composed of four wheels topped by a deck and pulled by a pony adorned with bells; above it, is lodged what seems to be an entire Egyptian family, the women with the long black robe and a veil that reaches to the eyes but does not hide the bottom part of the face, as it is made of lace.

The journeys from a place to another were quite regular and brought him a whiff of oxygen that helped him to bear the rough sides of his life.

If the trips towards Cairo were appreciated, other missions were harder to face, like the one of March 1941, on the other side of the canal.

The crossing of the Suez Canal is operated on two ferryboats which are not sufficient for traffic but also in a bad shape, and consequently are despairingly slow. Trucks, soldiers, Arabs, and camels are squeezed indiscriminately, no place is wasted on board, to the great discomfort of the camels, it seems.

At Kantara East, we had to wait till midnight for the only passenger train that connects Egypt to Palestine daily. Our destination was not Palestine though: Bir-El-Abd was a small railway station at about 75 kilometres from Kantara and distant from the coast by 8 kilometres approximately. We reached there at around 2 o'clock in the morning, and we settled down as best we could on the veranda of the station for the night. The next day, the camp was lifted and work started.

But barely started, as it had to stop in order to wait for a supply of materials. Needless to say, idleness in such a place was something terrible, add to that the inevitable discomfort in such circumstances.

The impossibility of taking a bath was one of the things that cost me most. The big distraction was the passage of the afternoon train. The whole camp rushed then towards the station in order to beg for a newspaper, a magazine, or whatever the passengers (generally soldiers or sisters) had the kindness to offer us.

In spite of the monotony of such a lifestyle, my stay at Bir-el-Abd provided me with new experiences. Camel treks, Arabic classes taught by Bedouins, studies -basic of course - of their customs, had at the beginning at least, the attraction of novelty.

The herds of black goats standing out in the whiteness of the sand, Arab women all black clad, and balancing a pottery on top of their head, caravans of camels moving in line slowly ...

Here are topics for someone more gifted than me! Maybe one day I shall try to describe what I have but only noted after appreciating the beauty.

In addition to the officers who accompanied me, I made the acquaintance of other persons.

I went several times to El Amish, a hospital for convalescents about 70 kilometres away; the officers had invited us to a Mass whenever we had the opportunity. Some of them were charming and deserved to be known. (...) The Catholic chaplain was a Benedictine monk, very young and outspoken, and with a remarkable open mind.

The atmosphere I met with at El Amish was such that I wanted to be sick in order to be sent there for recovery!

The following May, Hyacinthe was sent to another camp, at Marsa Matruh, on the Mediterranean coast, 300 metres away from the sea. *"A sea whose tones of blue and vast white beach reminds me of Mauritius,"* he wrote.

As usual, this new mission was a great comfort to him at first, but it soon turned into wretchedness. The camp was not far from town, which he described in many details in his notebooks.

The town extends towards our East, a rather big agglomeration of villas and small modern buildings, at some places, or in most cases quite similar to the types of buildings that are found everywhere in Egypt: cubes of masonry and clay, with no style except that of sand castles that children build for fun on the beach.

Between the sea and us lies a small hotel, the Lido Hotel, with quite a pleasant design, a large circular terrace extending towards the beach. Here and there, is a small mosque whose minaret raises a white arrow through the blue sky. But at sunset the muezzin does not come anymore with his daily lament, exhorting the faithful to prayer; and in the main street the boutiques have no more display to attract tourists.

Matruh, which a few months ago must have been a pleasant small town, with its straight-lined constructions and small gardens which must have been the pride of their owners, is now a fortified place.

Everybody has left, all the civilians at least, taking with them everything they could - some houses are ruined - Italian or German bombs - and, of those that are still up, all shelter soldiers.

I work at the motherent on the hill to the outh of the town - repairs and additions of roofs to water reservoirs. The works relating to water supply have been my only occupation till now. These works familiarize me with something absolutely novel to me.

The working days are quite busy: 8:00 to 12:30 , 13:00 to 16:30. On Sundays, two out of four sections take a rest. During afternoons, I usually go for a swim with Crossley and Fulton, an only way to be relatively clean in a place where soft water is rationed to one gallon per person and per day.

My only distractions are mail and reading. At the motherent I am reading *'The Egyptian promenade'* of Charles Aveline - interesting writing, well said; descriptions generally lively, sometimes romanticized. I cannot always share the author's point of view: maybe because we see Egypt under two different angles. These few words to remember about the pyramids: *'I will never tire of coming back to listen to the confidences of light.'*

The first trials he had to deal with were difficult relationships with his companions. His new boss irritated him considerably!

On top of his attitude which is typically 'sergeant' wise, he has a superior and arrogant tone which has always displeased me considerably. And yet I will have to tolerate him: one of the disadvantages of war that I had not known up till now.

He thought constantly of those who were so far and whose news was scarce. His birthday came - the first during these years of war, and he was inclined to feel sorry for himself.

I am 25 today - I received a cable from Mother yesterday, which gave me real pleasure. Birthdays have remained for me of the same importance since my childhood: the word has always remained as suggestive.

He tried then to hang on to:

The conviction that far from here, those whom I love are thinking of me at this very motherent. And why should I complain? Isn't this a sufficient reason to be happy?

He rejoiced at the arrival of German prisoners, which were encouraging signs of a progress towards the enemy lines. And a few days later, was devastated by the bad news that reached his ears. They were sometimes confusing and uncertain, but when relayed by the press, they seemed credible and trustworthy.

The news is growing more and more alarming. The newspapers announce today the loss of the Halfaya Pass on the Libyan front by our troops, and in Crete it seems that our army will not be able to resist any longer.

We have lost two 'cruisers' and four destroyers in the Mediterranean, as the R.A.F assistance to the navy is almost inexistent and the German troops continue to arrive in Crete.

My trust in our army and in the final victory is still there, but I cannot help wondering: where are our troops? What are they doing? About ten days ago Churchill declared we were about half a million in the Middle East, and I know that, since then, more troops have disembarked at Suez.

Hyacinthe analysed the virtues and limits of different troops around:

Until last week, the local garrison was composed of the Australian 7th division.

My experience with the Australian troops confirmed me what I had already heard about them. It is an army with no discipline at all – the officers have no power over their soldiers who treat them as equals – and who, owing to a propaganda that proves as false as noisy in the world press, think they are the best in the world.

If, to be a good soldier you have to dash down against an obstacle, without any reasoning, then Australia is the best. Even if this tactical plan has succeeded against the Italians, the recent events have shown that it is not the same with the Germans.

The South-Africans seemed much more disciplined than the Australians, and have made a better impression on me on the whole.

Also mentioned in his notebook, the presence of the second company of Mauritian pioneers, that of the Seychelles company, and that of the company of Palestine pioneers:

Among those, were a few interesting people, all Jewish and for the most part refugees from Germany or others occupied territories.

He finds himself among other nationalities: two sergeants, former lieutenants of Austrian Artillery, a corporal of Russian nationality, an engineer graduated at the University of California, who spoke, besides his mother tongue, English, French, German, Polish, and Hebrew.

Among the troop, there are Germans, Spanish, French, Polish, Palestinians - the extraordinary thing is that this Babel Tower seems to get along very well.

An important number of soldiers went to worship on Sunday morning.

I attended the 8:30 Mass this morning in the Greek Orthodox Church where Protestant Service or Catholic Mass follow each other every Sunday. Mass was celebrated by a Polish priest - even though the words were incomprehensible, I appreciated the low tone of the hymns. Impressive and comforting ceremony, I would even say, for I found that it helped to elevate the soul towards God and to find, close to Him, the comfort that is so necessary here.

God's disarmed his heart which had been trying to protect itself. The inner barriers fell, and he found himself totally hopeless, facing his poverty and abnegation, and the sacrifices that his soldier's condition imposed upon him:

Why am I so discouraged these days? I think that unconsciously I am influenced by the way of life that we lead here: no distraction (reading is not enough to change one's ideas), never any music (when I hear sounds that are more or less discordant from some accordion, I listen to them with delight), nothing but uniforms around me, no conversation that is unrelated to war, not even a feminine voice or a child's shout!

This is what my life is composed of - to this is added the bad news about Crete and the absence of letters from Mauritius (the last one from Eda reached me one month ago and the one from Mother five weeks ago!)

The atmosphere seems always oppressive. I feel that my endurance towards this existence, which is a perpetual constraint, is not going to last very long. Taylor has left on a vacation for two days - certainly he needed it more than any of us. He was looking very tired these two weeks, and the other officers and myself insisted that he should take a rest. I think that the arrival of Greenhill in our mess is one of the causes that contribute to my present state of discomfort and nervousness.

News from Mauritius was systematically subject to censure. He received Eda's letters pre-opened, and it was unbearable to know that their mails were always read in the offices by unknown employees.

He could not tell her everything, and obviously he did not even want to do so, as the news of war was bad.

Now that since a few days the Germans are totally masters of Crete, we can expect an intensive bombarding of Matruh at any time - general opinion is that the 'blitz' is not far away.

There's quite an important movement of troops in the town at the present time... I think that a huge British attack is due to be launched in the near future.. The news of Franco-German collaboration has been quite worrying for a few days now. What a shame for the French people this actual Darlan's policy!

While following the events in North Africa, Hyacinthe interested himself in what was happening in France and felt close to the French people. He could not stand the Petain regime. Minister Darlan had met Hitler several times and had announced his choice publicly: *'Germany will be victorious. If we do not collaborate with them, we shall be nothing. As to me, I choose collaboration.'*

I feel discouraged at this motherent: work slow-down, news from abroad is quite alarming (the Germans are gaining ground in Russia at a speed that I did not think possible), a mournful existence here, these are all causes for my current mindset. To this I should add Duncan's change of moods - previously always full of energy, always ready to laugh, he is now sad, pessimistic. Just as I was under the influence of his good mood, I am now affected by his sadness. I think that this is due to his health - the vacation that he took these days has not restored him completely.

In war, bullets, bombs and shells are needed to cause death or mutilate bodies; but not so much is needed to mutilate spirits, or alter characters. Here, we are not that close to the front - which rather recedes continually - we are in better security than many others, but the atmosphere is very heavy. I thought that a week off-duty would have changed my ideas but no! I feel older, and terribly empty: the enthusiasms, the optimism and the illusions that, I believe, are essential to one's well being, I feel that all that is leaving me, is going to be replaced by scepticism, by a disillusioned conception of life. My God, may all that be just temporary and may I find my true self again when this nightmare is gone!

Small consolations brought him comfort. Little nothings that in the desert were priceless!

The day before yesterday, evening concert at Lido Hotel: three 'bands' and a Polish Choir. (Military music, South African and popular songs by the South African and National Hymn by the Palestinians.) I had the pleasure to listen to the music for one hour and forget for a while the worries and the grief...

Some weeks later, he wrote about the music:

Since two days now, Duncan Taylor has returned to the Company - he brought a wonderful radio for the mess. What a joy now to hear music and also to receive the latest news! The thing runs almost non-stop!

If the musical notes pacified and comforted him, there was nothing to compare with a letter from the closest ones to make him happy. He mainly received letters from Eda and his mother.

Received this morning a letter from Eda that I read and reread, as is usual for the slightest mail received from Mauritius. My mail continues to reach me quite irregularly. I cannot find any explanation for these delays.

It pains me that apart from a word from Marc Lagesse, and a letter from Max I have received nothing from my friends since I am in Egypt. If only they could know the joy that a few words, even hastily scribbled, can bring, I am sure that they would make an effort to put an end to what is, I hope, mere negligence!

His daily prayer is of a sweet support to him. He mentions little of that, but a mark of a living relationship with God appears regularly in his notebooks. His comments about the Russians testify to this:

Are they really convinced atheists? And if they are, will they remain so forever? Is war not going to trigger a natural reaction against the anti-religious and amoral doctrines that a 'clique' of fanatics wants to impose on the people?

I learnt today that the Russian women were praying for their husband, father, brothers, who are facing the invader. Danger is bringing them back to the reality: that we are all in the hands of God and that on Him alone our destinies depend.

At Marsa Matruh, the violence of war was very close and prayer helped him to challenge the fear of bombs that often threatened.

The night before last, one of them fell at about 150 metres from me - explosion and mainly quite terrifying whistles. The worst is the uncertainty as to the place where the next will fall. Rather bad reaction from the company - especially from those who start to panic – a feeling amplified by a tragedy that occurred in the camp of a Mauritian Pioneers' company, two days ago. A bomb that fell in their camp caused panic, the aftermath of which led one of the members to hang himself.

In his eyes, each human being remained a sacred one, even in the enemy camp:

Saw an officer imprisoned in a special 'cage', separated from the soldiers, with his impressive stature, his air of condescending indifference, sitting on his woollen blanket under the hard-beating sun with his poor belongings around him; he distinctly offered a nice example of behaviour and dignity.

What thoughts hid beneath those looks fixed on the horizon? Was he a murderer, a bloodthirsty fanatic, or simply a father of a family exiled by war, who was dreaming of his wife, of his children?

If only men could understand each other and realize that God has not created Earth to turn it into a battlefield!

This comment flowed forth from his guts throughout all the adversary's assaults that occurred continuously in Egypt during the summer of 1941. War seemed more and more absurd to him!

The bombardments continue, quite violent; according to statistics, an average of 100 bombs are dropped every night in the past few months. The damages are astonishingly low, we could say: almost none. Two years now that we are at war with Germany; two years that this conflict has started, where the entire mankind, if not intimately involved, is indirectly engaged! It is a turmoil that destroys the work of so many years of human civilization.

Today we have to kill, kill as many enemies as possible! How sad to think that this is our goal!

Luckily Hyacinthe could take a few leaves that provided him some rest.

I obtained a leave this week and I shall depart tomorrow for Cairo. How good it will be, during a few days, to stop seeing these sandbags and iron masks, to sleep in a soft bed, enjoy a hot bath, rediscover the comfort that I have come to almost forget now!

During these moments of hindsight, the idea of doing something else, of trying to engage in a different way in the British Army started to take roots in his mind.

I have at this moment a project that I would like to put to execution: be an interpreter between the Free French forces and the English Army. I am certain unfortunately that, if such a post exists, there must be many more qualified than me to fill it (...).

I mentioned this idea to Duncan. He advised me to let it go, being of the opinion that it wasn't necessary to apply for a post where risks would surely be greater than those I face here.

It is not this point of view that would make me abandon my project but rather the prospect of leaving the company, which I care for, and especially Duncan. I know too that the latter would see me leave with distress, as, being both Mauritians, we speak often about the country, and he seems so exhausted and discouraged at the moment that having a compatriot here seems to be a support for him. These are the reasons that make me indecisive about what I shall do.

His friend Duncan was a great daily support, and his departure faced Hyacinthe with a deeper dilemma.

Today is certainly the saddest day I spent since my departure from Mauritius! Major Taylor, called back to Mauritius by a telegram, left us this morning. At the beginning of these notes I have written a few impressions of his character - it is therefore unnecessary that I describe his qualities once more. I would nevertheless like to add this: Duncan has become for me a true friend, and now that he is gone, I realize even more to what extent he was such. I may have an exaggerated sensitivity (a defect I try my best to correct) but as I shook his hand to say 'goodbye' this morning, I was too moved to speak. I have to say however that the pain caused by the Major's departure is mixed with the pleasure of seeing him return to his own.

Actually, more than ever, my impatience to see the advent of victory is increasing day by day.

But the victor which he was looking forward to was still far away, and he had to bear the daily life that was, finally, much different to that he had imagined when he had enlisted.

Life is more and more monotonous – a sheer existence that engenders boredom, and with boredom discouragement and that yearning for the country which comes back ever more furiously then. On this Saturday afternoon, after the heavy heat and the lack of activities of the day, among the flies that hardly allow me to write, how I measure my loneliness!

How can I overcome my sadness, prevent my thoughts from flying to Mauritius, towards Mother, towards Eda? A few years ago, I was probably at Sans Souci with Eda, quiet, happy, enjoying a happiness that is so far away now. And how long is this terrible war going to last? How many more afternoons like this one await me still?

My God, give me the courage without which I feel I cannot do anything!

The contact with the sea brought him some comfort but also contributed to nurture some homesickness.

The sea is not too far, but the sand hills do not allow me to see it. When the winds come from offshore, I hear them roar and the noise of the waves makes me forget for a motherent the present reality by sending me back to my native island.

As the end of the year 1941 approached, the notes became grimmer and sad. Difficulties succeeded each other, piled up, always heavy. Lack of work or difficult work, lack of news, health problems, lack of water, difficult relationships with his peers ... All these problems accumulated and gnawed at him like a cancer.

Around Christmas and New Year celebrations, he tried his best to go back over that first year of war. A year in the desert of Egypt had slowly produced in him an arid desert.

On the approach of the end of the year, together with Christmas and New Year, this neurasthenia that I had started to feel these past days is getting worse. The desire to be back home, with my own, is becoming an obsession. Nothing else interests me down here. I no longer speak to anyone unless if I have to, and rather seek refuge as long as possible in my room where, alone with my thoughts, I am better.

To add to my discouragement (or perhaps because of it?) my mail is very irregular: no letter from Eda, for these past ten weeks. When I see my friends receive letters and greeting cards, this increases my sorrow.

How much longer will I have to stay here? This is a question which no one would be able to answer but which I don't stop asking myself.

Today is Christmas Eve. How different from the 24th December that I have known till now, especially the last one! I have always kept this naive and childish enthusiasm for the celebrations around New Year, those moments when the family gathers together and when, in Mauritius, nature is also celebrating. 24th December is not yet Christmas, nor New Year, but it is even better: ultimate preparations, that are even more appreciated than the very motherent that we are all waiting for. Who is the philosopher who said: "I like nothing better than what is coming next."? But here in the desert of the West, the 24th December and the days that will follow are nightmares from which I hope to wake up as fast as possible.

Last day of 1941! Another year is ending, but a very special one this time, a year which will certainly leave an indelible mark upon the course of my existence.

Sitting at my small table in my makeshift room, contemplating my campaign bed, my iron mask, my gas mask, all the objects that are so familiar to me today, I can't help reflecting upon what my life has been during these last twelve months. And what strikes me is the speed with which the days have passed.

He will then make a summary of what has happened and comes to the following conclusion:

The few facts that I just mentioned only mark different steps along a year that has been the most original of my life so far.

I have known the sorrow of being separated from those I love the most in the world: I have seen countries or at least towns that differ from the ordinary: I have learnt to know people of diverse social ranks and nationalities; I have become acquainted with the army, the war time one, the only one which I am happy to be part of.

The raids, almost non-stop during six months, sometimes made me feel death at a hair's breadth; in a few words, I have experienced life considerably this last year; but I wonder also if, as a logical consequence, I have not aged a lot. The satisfaction of accomplished duty is however stronger than anything I may have lost by going to war. On the threshold of this year that is starting, my only wish is for a fast victory, and that I may be soon among my own.

Sitting in front of a cup of tea, Hyacinthe writes to better stick to the hope which supports him, to throw away, by means of ink on paper, this inner grime that was already destroying the first impetus of his generous enlisting.

He feels good when supping tea while writing, even if he sees – even in this faithful drink – but binding forces.

It is a drink that varies both in appearance and taste: sometimes of the same color as coffee and milk, or otherwise of a brownish red, more like chocolate. Can be transparent at times, or otherwise with a surface as shiny as a soup.

Usually it tastes like chlorine, but more often the dust flavour is quite stronger. This morning, it was more like tobacco; at other times it reminds me of the tea which we had in Sinaï: the water was probably coming out of a locomotive boiler, or goat milk with a rather pungent savour. But never ever have I met with a look or a taste that deserves the true name by which everybody refers to tea.

The Promised Land

Eda had enrolled in the Red Cross in Mauritius. She handled the parcels that were sent for the necessities of war. She also formed part of the team that trained the public, on the one hand to react in a convenient way in case of attack, and on the other hand, to be able to provide first aid in case of necessity.

This enrolment brought her closer to her fiancé, who was constantly in her thoughts, sometimes with much apprehension. When, being at home, she saw Georges Wiehe's car or another close relative of Hyacinthe's approach, she jumpstarted and shivered, wondering if it did not bring her bad news. She sometimes dreaded the worst.

The letters that she wrote regularly did not always reach the right destination. Some were mysteriously lost, others were scattered among large numbers at the Censorship office. Connection between the two fiancés was quite complicated. Hyacinthe was often crushed down by a mental anguish.

The absence of news from Mauritius is felt more and more every day: from Eda I have not received any letter for three months now. It is not merely sadness that overwhelms me: now neurasthenia is impacting on all my activities.

Before the war, suffering was something quite far from Uncle Hyacinthe's daily life. He had seen it sometimes in his relatives, had felt it now and then sneaking around like a stray dog. Sometimes it had bitten him. But these past trials were largely compensated by the sweetness of the family surroundings and the Mauritian atmosphere, by the warmth of these relations, so affectionate, with the members of his family, in particular with his mother and his fiancée.

This first year of war was in reality a year spent in taming suffering. It had introduced itself into all the little details of his daily life, becoming progressively his faithful companion, his daily bread.

At first, these trials seemed easily overcome. He delved into his mental resources in order to face and conquer them. He also had proper time to pull himself together between two trials. But slowly, as the months passed, suffering infiltrated itself everywhere, in the slightest fissure of his heart, like water that spreads out and finds a way, fearing no obstacle, as big as it may be.

When mental suffering appears in someone's history, when it is a vehicle for a sort of venom, back and forth first, then imposing itself, what is the normal reflex? What is the spontaneous reaction of a normally constituted human being? Doesn't he try to escape? Doesn't he decide to get away as far as possible, to hide, to slip into oblivion, so that the suffering stops harassing him and throwing him off balance?

Thus was Hyacinthe's reaction, as he was undergoing these trials. Since his tender childhood, he had had the opportunity to choose sacrifices voluntarily: fasting, privations, efforts upon oneself, etc.

But, when he did it, it was always with the possibility of deciding on the duration of these sacrifices. There he chose the beginning and the end. Here, in the middle of the desert impossible to choose! He underwent all prevailing sufferings, and felt that he had not enough resources to handle them, that his endurance was limited. The only space where he could take refuge was his soul. But this also had grown into an infertile soil.

To desert the army was not a solution, because he had a sense of honour and of duty. Therefore, out of a survival reflex, he looked for another resort. The only one that seemed realistic was to pass on to a different activity, at all costs!

Yesterday, Lieutenant Hurlin, a French engineer, came for supper and night here. He came from Halfaya, looking for explosives. He is from Lorraine, his birthplace is Metz, and he spent a long time in Cameroon before the war.

I chatted with him quite a long time; there is a feeling of sadness and discouragement that comes from his conversation - sadness at the thought of the recent past and present states of France, and discouragement as to its future.

"France is a doomed country!" he told me.

Through him, I learn that the Free French Movement is a lot less important than what I thought: barely 10,000 soldiers, not all of whom are well trained.

After my conversation with Hurlin, I ask myself if it would not be worth the trouble for me to be a liaison officer or an interpreter with De Gaulle's army - for I have decided since some time now to offer my services again, my first letter of candidature having probably not reached the headquarters.

In spite of all, I don't think of coming back on my decision. Our mess has become hateful to me, although I realize that it is probably better than many others. There reigns an atmosphere of contained animosity among the different members, a sentiment of hypocrisy that I cannot bear.

Perhaps it is my own fault that I am unhappy, because I create my own worries or at least I amplify those that I would have been able to leave behind. But truly, I cannot overcome by sheer reasoning this feeling of sadness that crushes me under its weight. One single thought dwells in me: to return among my own.

3 March 1942

Life goes on, quite monotonous these days. Work, not interesting, is abundant at this time. I have no longer any time left to read or study as I would have liked. I am still waiting for the result of my candidacy for a transfer; the application has been recommended by Colonel Edmunds; I wish that my hopes are not illusions.

What worries me more and more is the situation in the East. It seems that the Japanese will soon occupy Java. Despite the reassurances of the Vichy Government, won't the next step be Madagascar? I prefer not to think of that, for what would happen to Mauritius then! It is hard to be separated from one's own, on conditions that are not always pleasant, but the isolation, the danger, the discomfort are bearable when one knows that those one loves are safe in the background. But when this conviction starts to fade, one has to be very strong to avoid discouragement. At the present time I do not even have a letter from Mauritius; from Eda I have been deprived of any direct news since two months.

I do not hesitate to say that it is not the least trial of the war. In such moments, more than others, I am happy to be a Christian and to be able to pray.

Prayer was always a resource that, by presenting it to God, helped to diminish his sufferings. The Psalms, which constitute the basis of Christian prayer, inspire the words that allow each one to cry out to Heaven, to express supplication, to renew one's faith in the One who created us.

I cried out to God for help;
I cried out to God to hear me.
When I was in distress, I sought the Lord;
at night I stretched out untiring hands,
and I would not be comforted.
I remembered you, God, and I groaned;
I meditated, and my spirit grew faint.[b]
You kept my eyes from closing;
I was too troubled to speak.
I thought about the former days,
the years of long ago;
I remembered my songs in the night.
My heart meditated and my spirit asked:
"Will the Lord reject forever?
Will he never show his favor again?
Has his unfailing love vanished forever?
Has his promise failed for all time?
Has God forgotten to be merciful?
Has he in anger withheld his compassion?"

(Psalm 77)

Did the Psalms sustain Hyacinthe's prayer? Maybe not, but owing to his sensitivity and love of poetry, with his spontaneity, he surely found words similar to the ones of the Sacred Texts. Among different prayers, any way, one of them was particularly dear to him: The Rosary. He had been marked by the attitude of a priest he had met one day, and who had suggested to him to hang on to it firmly, to persevere patiently.

5 March 1942

Today I receive a letter of Father Arrowsmith whom I have known in the Sinai. He obtained my address from one of our men, and, very kindly wrote to me and sent a Rosary that he had placed on the Rock of Agony, at Gethsemani and also on the Calvary and the Holy Sepulchre.

By what inspiration had that priest tried to trace Hyacinthe? He must certainly have met many soldiers since the beginning of the war, but he kept a few in his memory, in his prayers.

This good chaplain had simply three things at heart: first of all, support Hyacinthe by a brotherly gesture by writing him a little word of encouragement and comfort. Then, with sensitivity, by inviting him to pray persistently.

During war, every object has its importance and one cannot afford the luxury of going around, with unnecessary or decorative items. The Rosary that was sent to him was therefore a clear invitation. And finally, this Rosary had been laid in two places: the Rock of Agony and that of Calvary. Two places marked by Jesus-Christ's suffering, rejected by men but victorious over evil, by the love with which he lived his Passion for the welfare of mankind.

It was an important message that doubtlessly Hyacinthe could not understand immediately, nor maybe anticipate its value. That Rosary was the weapon with which he would vanquish suffering, the weapon for a recovery that would transform him slowly in the very depth of his being.

A few weeks later he made this pertinent remark:

It is one year since I have been at Marsa Matruh, a year which, despite sadness and loneliness, and worries, has flied. Time seems to pass so quickly that I wonder if it is not a special grace that God gives us - a grace that not only renders the hours less time consuming but gives courage to face adversity more easily.

Following the inspiration of his soul, he prayed with that strong intuition and that sweet certainty that his prayer was not in vain, that God had not abandoned him but on the contrary that He remained close, upholding his steps. That weapon of the Rosary did not abandon him, but he was a soldier and had also to learn to handle weapons of war.

15 March 1942

This afternoon I leave for Geneifa, to follow a course of 10 days on the way to 'defuse' the unexploded bombs, and to dispose of them. The knowledge on that subject has to be shared among the Engineering Department and I believe the course is interesting. This morning we had rifle-shooting exercises. The major part of the company is armed with Italian rifles, which are appalling according to what we have been able to see: they lack precision, and, as to their quality, they are not comparable to English ones.

After this short period of formation and training, he received the reply he had been waiting for with such eagerness, but which was negative.

29 March 1942 - Marsa Matruh

I return to Marsa Matruh this morning. My course ended with an exam I have passed quite successfully. I stop at Cairo for one day on my way, just to cut the long journey in two.

At my arrival I learn what I was already dreading: I am not accepted as liaison officer. "The officers with experience and knowledge cannot be liberated from their Mauritian Engineering Company", says the letter of reply to my candidacy. It is a disappointment, a big disappointment, I must confess. But since such a duty is imposed on me by the circumstances, I just have to accept the situation and make the best of it. Isn't it the only way to be happy - or at least, not to be unhappy: accept without bitterness what cannot be avoided?

In the afternoon I attend the funeral of Tom who commanded a section of the Engineering Company: he was killed yesterday while clearing a minefield. I had known him last year and he was quite a good friend of mine. I remember the photos of his mother and sister he showed me at that time, and it is of them that I think today. Yes, those whom we leave back in our country have certainly more to suffer than we do!

Quite resigned, he took time to digest the news. But, as soon as another opportunity presented itself, he tried again his chance, hoping to turn to something new, and above all, to put an end to this untenable situation.

23 April 1942

Monday, following a circular letter from the commander in chief, I applied to be transferred to India. Transfer applications are purely voluntary among the Egyptian troops and the 8th Army.

I have many reasons for having proposed my services for this endeavour: see a country other than Egypt of which, after more than a year in the desert, I am starting to get tired, to be involved in jobs that seem more interesting or instructive than those I have to do here; to earn probably a higher salary than the one I earn here; perhaps to have the chance to go on leave to Mauritius in a short time, and above all, to respond to the call of the Commander-in -chief.

All these reasons, not listed by way of preference, have pushed me to take this decision. I hope that this time I will be luckier.

Happiness! That is what he missed mostly, and that he hoped to retrieve as fast as possible, with no difficulty whatsoever! Happiness! One cannot reproach him this yearning for such a precious objective, the one to which we all aspire. But at this time, his vision of happiness could not co-exist with suffering. The two were incompatible for him.

At times, he could escape to the seaside and enjoy long moments of meditation, a bit like the old days in Mauritius.

A little bit, as both were really incompatible.

3 May 1942

It is good to dream at dusk, at the time when light is leaving and darkness falls. It is good to dream and recall memories that the increasing darkness calls forth; parade of joys and tears! The sun has disappeared behind the sand dunes, the sea loses its scale of nuances: the luminous green transparency turns into opaque blue.

And the short wavelets, in a constant repeated move, lap the white sand shore continuously: murmurs blending with the loud lapping of the sea. But no familiar sound accompanies the waves' complaint: where are the lamentations of the tall filaos that bend down and weep in the breeze?

Where are the songs of birds, invisible in the greenery, say *adieu* to the vanishing day?

And is it all that I miss? I don't see anymore the green and dense grass that pushes through the rocks, nor the big white clouds enlightened by a last ray of light. I don't smell the strong scent of marine algae the breeze mixes with the logwoods' penetrating perfume. And above all, there are beside me no dear ones to comfort me by their presence. Parade of memories, carry on!

But a reality superimposes itself to the dream. It is the bay of Marsa Matruh that I see among the date-trees. Clumps of greyish date-trees, dried up by the scorching sand winds and the sun. The ground on all sides is holed, bloated by the trenches, by the shelters, by a few bomb craters.

Some sand bags properly aligned in certain places, scattered and torn apart in others. Camouflage filets lying upon all kinds of vehicles, and further, on the very edge of the sea, the Lido, also hurt to death and marked with scars: big openings without windows, cracks along the walls, collapsed steps, and on the roof, a power-gun pointing towards the sky.

And now, the sinister call of the siren, quick! Iron cask and trench! The Fritz planes are here!

On 28 June we got the order to evacuate Matruh: the fortress had to be defended by the New Zealand division and some other troops. On the 29, at dawn, the company was leaving, partly by truck and partly on foot - as we had not enough vehicles to transport all the men and the materials.

The trucks had to move on a shift system in order that everyone would have an equal distance to walk - our target was Alamein, at about 110 miles to the east.

Soon after departure, I realized what a nightmare the voyage was going to be. The road was a moving mass of vehicles, a river of trucks, tractors, cars, that knocked each other, passed each other, ran into each other, stopped sometimes, when the jam became inextricable, and started again in the same rush towards the East. And I thought then that this movement of troops had not even reached the stage of a "strategic withdrawal", for no carriage or canon had started yet to come down!

These expressions can by no means be understood by anyone who has never, ever, seen what I am talking about!

And so, dragged away by that sort of current, we arrived - after many a stop on the way to reassemble the troops and reorganize the movement - in Alamein, in the evening of the same day. There, it seemed that we had reached a flat land where we could stay for some time without leaving the lines of communication with our operation zone. But the next day we learnt that the Germans were midway between Sid-Barrani and Marsa Matruh, and two days after, news came to us that Matruh was under siege.

On the main road that dominated our camp, the train of convoys fleeing the enemy continued to pass by: the exodus to the East, like a fresco on move, enhanced against the bright background of the summer sun or against the colorless sky of a too-pale moonlight. I often thought of what bloodshed the enemy could have caused, was its aviation sufficiently strong to attack such a target.

This strategic withdrawal marked a step in the Middle East war during this period. The current situation was evolving and, taking advantage of a period of respite, Hyacinthe went to Palestine for the first time in September of that same year,

This voyage was a turning point during his war years, like a first exploration of a place where he was going to live during many months in the future.

We are in 1942. At that time, the country was under British protectorate since the division of that part of the world by France and England in 1916. Its population consisted in majority of Palestinian Arabs, mostly Muslims, but also Christians. Quite an important population of Jews also resided there, some since many generations.

A great number of them were refugees, due to the prevailing Shoah in Europe. Many had arrived before 1939, influenced by a Zionism that advocated a return to the Promised Land and the creation of a State for the Jewish people, scattered around the world for more than 1900 years.

In 1947 the United Nations Organization was going to decide in favour of splitting the country so as to allow the Jews to have their own nation. And it was in 1948 that the State of Israel was to be created.

Uncle Hyacinthe therefore discovered this country at the time when a great historical turning point was in preparation. No violent confrontation between the Jews and the Palestinians was noted. Some tensions erupted at times, but the British mandate succeeded in favouring social peace, a bit fragile surely, but quite evident.

This being said, in this context of world war, it was rather the political situation in Europe that worried everybody, and occupied all minds. Upon arrival in Palestine, Hyacinthe was going to experiment more than a voyage: mostly a pilgrimage.

For any Christian, this land is called Promised Land, since we believe that here, in this corner of the planet, God came down to live with us during 33 years. Folly of Christianity! Scandal for some! Aberration for others! But this is what inhabited the heart and intelligence of the one who had grown up in the Catholic faith.

This pilgrimage to the source of Christianity was an unexpected motherent, but so much welcome at this stage of his enlistment in the army.

While he was consumed by a yearn to escape from the desert, this was an occasion to immerge into the Gospel by going to the places where the events concerning the life, but also the death and the resurrection of Jesus-Christ had taken place.

Jerusalem, 29 September 1942

Yesterday afternoon, I left Cairo by train for Jerusalem. Crossing of the Suez Canal by the new port in the vicinity of Ismailia. Arrival at Lydda early this morning. There I meet my fellows: tourists, some non commissioned officers and soldiers.

A one-hour journey by car from Lydda to Jerusalem - landscape quite different from Egypt - succession of valleys and hills up which run the winding roads, pine woods wailing in the breeze, small villages upon hilltops.

I come down from San Remo, a little pension lodge to which I will have to get use for one day. I first take a tour of the Jewish quarters in the Old City - we enter by the Jaffa Gate and engage in a labyrinth of dirty and foul-smelling streets, most of which are covered by a stone arch.

Now the Church of the Holy Sepulchre: from the outside one sees more scaffoldings than stones, as it has been necessary to reinforce the walls that threatened to crumble down.

At the door I leave my group, as the guide's chitchat annoys me, to go and speak to a Franciscan monk, who guides me through the Sanctuary.

Four religions share the Holy Place: Roman Catholics, Greeks, Copts, and Armenians.

At the entrance, marble slabs covering the stone on which was embalmed the body of Our Lord: further, the Altar where is encased the Pole of Flogging; mosaic pavement indicates the place where Our Lord has accepted the offering of perfumes from Mary Magdalene; the Holy Sepulchre itself, embedded, if we can say that, in a building which is so full of ornaments that we can see nothing; the cave where were buried the three crosses after the Crucifixion. The Calvary, also lined with stones and marble, of which one sees only a small piece of rock on the top. The last three Stations of the Cross are found in the part reserved for the Catholic Church, whereas the very site of the Cross of Our Lord and of those of the two thieves, belong to the Greek Church.

In the section belonging to the Catholic Church is found a statue of the Virgin Mary, literally covered with offerings, all kinds of jewels.

I leave the Holy Sepulchre, struck by the fact that for too many people, it is more a historical site than a holy Place. The priest to whom I share my impressions says that indeed the visitors' attitude is not always respectful, but that one cannot do anything about it. But another feeling is that in the course of centuries, there has been so much building works, and accumulation of marble stones adorned with silver and gold, in a most Holy Place, the cradle of our religion, that now, it is completely disfigured or rather entirely hidden to our eyes. Why didn't they leave the hill of Calvary, the Holy Sepulchre, as they were twenty centuries ago? Wouldn't it have been much better, then, to pray in front of the scene that the Lord had himself contemplated or where he had suffered?

Nearby, a church could have been built equally beautiful, with as much ornaments as would be fit for such a sanctuary.

But why waste time in such considerations, when it is now too late to change anything!

A visit to the church of Saint Anne: silent and prayerful yard, shade of willows on the pavement, tall cypresses, both majestic and grim like candles.

In a corner of the yard, an old White Father was reading his Breviary: Inside, Seminarians attending to their prayers and devotions. Underneath the choir, here is the grotto where the Holy Virgin Mary was born. In front of the church, behind a wall, one finds the pool of Bethesda.

The Via Dolorosa: tortuous and tiring circuit which starts at 'Ecce Homo', which we follow to the eighth station, and that I climb with difficulty! And it is along this way that Our Lord, flogged, crowned with thorns, bore a heavy cross up towards the Calvary, in order to die for us!

1 October 1842

Yesterday morning I paid a visit to Bethlehem. The place where the Child-Jesus was born is under an altar belonging to the Armenians. On the side, a Catholic Altar is placed above a reproduction of the Crib, the original of which is in Rome. Further, at the end of a corridor, St Joseph's room; other altars are placed in different parts of the underground, for all this is found under the church, many times demolished and rebuilt during the course of history.

The Greeks and the Armenians share the administration of the big church; the Catholics own only a passage, in front of the Armenian Altar, leading from the stable to the Church of Nativity, and leaning on the other building.

This passage is carefully bounded by means of carpets placed on the marble floor. And in order to bring calm and order among members of the different religions, a Muslim policeman walks to and fro.

The Catholic Church of Nativity, from which Christian Masses are broadcasted, is a relatively recent construction, except for certain details.

Soon after my return to Jerusalem, I depart to Damascus by road. Passing through several villages, one of which is Nablus, close to which is found the Well of Jacob. Stop for lunch at Tiberiade, on the shores of the Sea of Galilee.

On the way, Jewish allotments, small farms with lands that seem well cultivated. Stop at the frontier for luggage control, crossing of 'no-man's land', and then we are in Syria.

The inhabitants seem to draw poor benefits from the water resources for their plantations; many lands near the rivers are infertile or produce poor cultures. After the border, outfits have changed, (...) after about nine hours of travel, arrival in Damascus, whose houses huddle together in the middle of a cluster of trees or climb up the mountainside. French caserns, soldiers with Poilu's helmets, French signposts, so many things that I had never seen during this war, and which please me.

After a stay in Damascus then in Beyrouth, Hyacinthe came back towards Jerusalem by following the Mediterranean Sea till Tel Aviv.

Before taking his trip back to Egypt, he took time to go to Mass and to write to his mother who was celebrating her birthday.

7 October 1942

My very dear Mother, I don't need to tell you that today my thought goes towards you in a very special way. This morning I attended Mass for you at the Church of Holy Saviour in Jerusalem, where I am since yesterday. May God bless you and give you the graces you need! My trip in Palestine and in the Levant is now drawing to its close...

As he took his notebook some days later:

Now the journey is over. 18 horrible hours of railway have brought me back to Cairo, covered with dust, tired and in a bad mood.

In some minutes, it will be the return to camp. During a few days I could have forgotten I was at war.

He had managed to forget the war, as well as the torments that had crushed him. But he had meditated on other sufferings: those of Jesus-Christ. Those places where he had walked remained engraved in his memory, and he was as if pacified by them.

Only some days after his return to camp, he learnt to his great surprise, what he had not at all expected! He had dreamt of change, had prayed for the end of his mission in the desert, begging Heaven to allow him to pass on to something else, that would attribute more meaning to his enrolment and which would irrigate his inner desert! The news arrived like a balm that allowed him to regain self-control and recover a taste for life.

I came back yesterday from Abbasia to learn that we are leaving tomorrow for Palestine. What a pleasant surprise to go in that direction rather than towards the sand plains of the western desert. The bulk of the company will go towards their new destination by train.

I arrive at Haifa on the 29 after 20 hours by railway. The company is a 'transit camp' to the South of the city and will stay there till the end of the week. We shall then leave for Transjordan where we have to take over from another company who is leaving for Egypt.

As far as I know, we shall be stationed on the banks of the Lake of Galilee, not very far from Tiberiade.

The company arrives here on the 6th. A rail journey, more than two hours long. Landscape quite pleasant along the route: little colonies of Jews in the midst of well cultivated fields, but gradually the soil seems poorer as we advance towards the East. The more fertile parts of the country seem to belong to the Jews, whereas the Arabs own the mediocre lands. The latter seem more primitive in their agricultural methods, using a wooden plough that was used thousands years ago, whereas, on the other side, in the Jewish part, only agricultural tractors and other mechanical instruments are seen.

I am disappointed by the Jordan, which, at the point where I cross it, is not even as wide as certain rivers in Mauritius.

Immediately after crossing the frontier we arrive at our camp: some caserns of 'Transjordan frontier force', for the most part actually unoccupied. The camp is situated on the plateau bordered, to the East and to the West, by chains of hills. But it is hard to believe that we are at 600 feet beneath sea level, except for a particular oppression in the atmosphere. But perhaps this is just our imagination.

To the North, the plateau descends quite abruptly towards a small artificial lake, crossed by the Jordan. We are South of Lake of Galilee, about 20 kilometres South of Tiberiade. My imagination had given an aspect of pomp and grandeur to that place, but in this little Jewish town, where a messy group of small constructions made of grey stones surround a few old fortifications, the reality seems quite different to me.

But let us return to our camp. On the border of the lake, at the top of the cliff, are a few bungalows representing the 'officers' mess'. Small constructions buried in the greenery, opening their verandas all wide unto lawns that may be tiny, but so fresh and so restful!

In front of my door, a cluster of yews adds a sad note to the solitude that surrounds us. And from my window I would be able to pick fruits from the trees that give shade to the house.

There is also a poultry yard where ducks and hens harmonize their discordant concerts tirelessly. So many sounds and shows that I had forgotten! One must have been in the nudity of the desert to understand their meaning.

The company continued to hang on to the news that arrived each day, and which some times brought a little comfort:

And now here is the superb performance of the French sailors of Toulon who sacrifice their lives by voluntarily sinking their ships! An act of courage that comes perhaps a bit too late - not enough, however, to remind those who doubted in France that the traditions of its Marine survive the shameful acts of its governing bodies.

Here, in the mess everyone has been full of admiration when the radio announced the events of Toulon, and the major has immediately proposed a toast to the French Navy. Will History one day solve the mysteries of this war?

The news of France awakened in him the sensitive issue of his own identity.

We spend a night in Beyrouth; there, the food and drink rations seem almost non-existent to one who has been in Palestine or even in Egypt – bread, especially, is excellent.

In the city, more French uniforms than English ones are seen; relationship between the two armies haven't seemed to me to be more than correct; I mean that there is no such thing which could be called brotherhood. The situation can, I believe, be summarized this way: the English consider the French in actual fact as their dependents (I don't use the word 'inferior' since, to the English eyes, it applies to everything that does not come from the United Kingdom) and the French strongly begrudge such an attitude.

I cannot imagine a human force that could completely fill the gap between the two countries' mentalities. We, Mauritians, are those who shall always suffer from that situation if we wish to remain faithful to our principles: keep the language, the culture, the religion of ancestors whom we are so proud of, while behaving as loyal members of the King and of the Empire. As to me, I am not ready to forsake such ideas, whatever the cost. But I am treading a path where I prefer not to take my pen...

Those questions about one's identity touch such deep and mysterious zones!

Who was he?

Who was he? A Mauritian of French descent, or a member of the British Empire?

Even his usual forename had changed since his enrolment in the army; he was henceforth called by the first of his first names, Jean or more often John, being immersed in an Anglo-Saxon environment.

He thus, while in Palestine, signed accidentally a letter to his mother. He would have to explain himself later, but maybe it was a sign of Providence, which referred him back to his first patron-saint: John the Baptist.

He had meditated on this point of the Gospel while journeying along the shores of the Jordan and other parts of Holy Land. John the Baptist proclaimed about Jesus-Christ: "*He has to grow and I have to diminish!*"

It was this program that awaited Hyacinthe, and what he no doubt felt within his soul.

He had felt diminished by trials and suffering. But he was starting to discern that it was perhaps a positive factor to give priority to the One who was to illuminate his life and confer a meaning to it.

He had wanted to escape from suffering, to try to get rid of it. Finally, while meditating on Christ's suffering, he would be receiving a gift of higher virtue.

But New Year was getting close. It was a new stage, always difficult to get through.

Jerusalem – 1st January 1943

1942 is gone - another year of war - another year in exile. Human beings continue to kill each other with even more obstinacy since the last three months.

How act otherwise, when all our deeds are but a response to the enemy, and when it is the only way to obtain victory? Will it happen this year, the little victory that we are looking forward to with such impatience? I can but only hope for it - experience has now tempered my last year's exaggerated optimism.

I begin the year by a monotonous working day at the camouflage school of Jerusalem where I follow a course. For the first time of my life I work on 1st January.

Where are the family celebrations with the children assembled, the season of flamboyant and lychee trees, the time when everybody seems so happy?

He found more opportunities to meet priests who were present on the holy sites, at Jerusalem or in the country.

Yesterday, I had lunch at Tiberiade at the convent of the Franciscan Sisters, visited by Father Mariano. The Father likes the 741 Company a lot, and we are almost friends. It is a pleasant change to lunch in the small refectory of the convent, with its wooden benches and its wax cloths tables.

There is only Father Mariano, plus two brothers, and an old Italian Father, recently out of concentration camp. The poor old man seems to ramble a little - and I am not sure that he was much pleased to see my British officer uniform.

The meal was excellent, consisting amongst all dishes, of fish from the Sea of Galilee, maybe the same fish that Our Lord distributed at the multiplication of the loaves.

This makes me realize once more how the Gospels are easier to follow and to remember when one knows the country.

Thus, from a burning desire to return to his native country, Hyacinthe was finally led to the Promised Land, the Holy Land, the place where geography re-awakens catechism's teachings and stories heard, but with one inattentive ear only.

This phase in Palestine was a period of consolation and a major turning point during his years of enlistment in war.

Parachutist

Among his numerous attempts, at all costs, to move on to another area, Hyacinthe had taken time to respond to the appeal launched by the Chief of Staff to join the parachutist corps. He had waited during long months for a reply that seemed to have been lost.

He received it eventually, at the time when he had stopped thinking about it A positive reply: his candidacy had been approved!

Hyacinthe was happy to see a new horizon unfurling at last:

On the 28 February great news arrived: news of an event which opens a new chapter in my existence: I have been accepted in a squadron of parachutists.

Sunday morning the major rushes into my room, his hand extended towards me, and, without giving me time to understand what is happening, tells me: *"Congratulations, John! You have been posted to 'F' Parachute Squadron!"*

My first reaction has been astonishment - astonishment that my nomination had been carried out so fast, without any medical examination, nor any other formality.

After the first motherent of surprise, the feelings changed into a mixture of satisfaction, regret and resignation: satisfaction for being nominated to a new post where one has the sensation to contribute more to victory, regrets to leave a company to which I am attached more than I thought, resignation at the thought that I am embarking now in a path where the expected effort is great and where the risks are overwhelming.

No joy, no real pleasure when I present myself on the threshold of this new career, the dangers which I have anticipated from the beginning - dangers which appear only more real now that their shadow seems to envelop me already.

I say: no pleasure, for many people will perhaps be of the opinion that I am jumping, with a joyous serenity, into a great adventure, adventure whose most probable conclusion is death. But does the opinion of the majority count much? The most important thing for me is that Mother and Eda know that in acting in this way, I have neglected nothing to fulfil my duty. I have no need to reassure them that I love them more than ever, while the risks of never seeing them again have so much increased. I leave them to be the only judges of my conduct and I know well that I have their approval.

Immediately after having been accepted, he was meditating on the risks of dying during combat. He felt at peace, because inhabited by a strong desire to offer his life for victory, in a useful way. But he could not help thinking of his own, and in particular of his mother and his fiancée.

He wrote to his mother on 10 March 1943:

My very dear Mother, my new address will be for you a first indication of the decision that I have taken for a while now. Indeed, I am now a parachutist - or rather I am on the way of becoming one if everything goes well.

Since December, when the authorities have made an appeal for volunteers in this service, I have proposed. The reason that has led me to take this decision is neither a taste nor a particular inclination for this kind of occupation. I have only thought that since volunteers are needed, I have no sufficient reason for not being among them.

I hope, or rather I know, my dear Mother, that I have your approval for what I just did. Maybe some people will criticize me: please tell them on my behalf that I have no use for the comments of those who have no right to judge me. Above all, I would not like to be taken for a hero.

I count also on you, my dear Mother, to have a talk with Eda about all this. She, too, has not yet been kept informed of my decision, and it is only today that I shall write to her. I know very well that she will approve of me - but I also understand that it will be difficult for her to grow used to the idea - especially at the beginning.

Hyacinthe was conscious more than ever that his life was at stake. He knew that death could be the conclusion of his enrolment with the parachutists. But his motivation was clear: he did not seek to be a war hero or to please himself. He had heard a call from the General Staff, and this call had met with his desire to move on to something else.

Certainly, in his desire for a change, there was also a part of yearning for an escape, of a search for a certain appeasement. But time did its work, and having been accepted in the squadron of parachutists, he retrieved the first enthusiasm that had brought him to join the war: offer his life in sacrifice in order that England and France recovered their freedom.

His mother's and Eda's reactions arrived. In the following letter that he addressed to his mother, he thanked her for her response:

I thank you for having gone to see Eda and for having talked to her about my change of function: I also have to thank you, my dear Mother, for having accepted my decision that way. I realize that the South-African priest was right when he said that we should realize that during war, it was above all our parents who had to suffer. Today, I also received a letter from Eda, who, as I expected, takes the news with a lot of resignation; nevertheless, I can read between the lines how much she is affected.

Moascar, 14 March 1943

Yesterday it has been a week since I arrived at Moascar in order to join the '4th Parachute Squadron'. It is with many regrets and much emotion that I have left the 741.

How could it be otherwise when I spent more than two years in this company? Two years during which I learnt to know everyone, to command and help those I was in charge of; two years during which I shared with the same men, the same sorrows, the same dangers, the same anxieties. Departure from Mauritius, bombardments in the desert, exile that seemed endless, I did not suffer from them alone; all that got me closer to those who were enduring them with me.

If the troops that I was commanding were quite different from me by their social and cultural level, or their mentality, they were after all men like me and the common dangers made me appreciate them more than I did in the civilian life.

They seemed all so sad to see me leave that I could not help being quite moved when I left them. I do not try to overestimate my merits: I have only done what any other Mauritian officer would have in my place - and perhaps better than me. Also, it was not without sadness that I left the officers of the company. If I flipped through these notes, I would certainly find more than one page where I complained about the heterogeneity of our mess, of the different idiosyncrasies that could not be harmonized, or certain defects in some of them that I could not get used to. This does not prevent the fact that I appreciated everyone, one way or another, and that I realize that I miss them.

After these few words on the subject of my departure, I should now speak about my arrival here. The 4th Parachute Squadron is presently at Moascar.

Upon my arrival, I had an interview with the major commanding the squadron, a man called Hardiman, regular soldier, all filled with defects and qualities of his kind.

The result of this interview was deplorable: I came out with the impression that my training in military engineering was totally inadequate to fill my new functions, and that it would be better to go back to a post that I could fill in a satisfactory manner.

I started feeling really unhappy, almost as much as at the time of the worst difficulties that I had had to face.

After a second interview with the major, it had even been almost decided that I would return to the 741. Obviously, all this was not at all inspired by a sudden fear of the danger of my new post: I had anticipated those dangers much before then, but I thought maybe I had under-estimated the difficulties of the kind of work that was expected of me.

I should mention that even if I had no fear about training as a parachutist, what I saw upon arrival was not meant to reassure me: one of the officers just broke his collar bone, another had smashed his knees and a third had been killed with a skull fracture. But I repeat: it was certainly not that which frightened me.

Once the shock of this first contact passed, I started to realize that I would most probably be able to fill my new post - or at least try until proof of my inability.

I suppose that this change in my opinion was caused by the comradeship and cordiality that prevailed among the officers. They assured me that I should not attach importance to what Hardiman had told me, and that I should stay in the squadron.

I realized that the difficulties that I was facing were surely not insurmountable, and that it would be nice to live among these companions, all so much younger than me - in general they were between nineteen and twenty-three years old. I should add that if most of them have welcomed me with great affability, some others keep their distance and their sense of superiority which popular belief has made an Englishman's quality, but which is too often exaggerated until it becomes a defect. In their eyes I probably had an 'inferiority complex', those words so dear to the inhabitants of the United Kingdom and so much used in a sense that goes widely beyond the limits of their meanings. But I would not like to embark on a subject that I would like one day, given the chance, to write about.

30 March 1943

After a fortnight stay in Egypt, at the camp of Moascar, I am returning to Palestine.

The 4th Parachute Brigade has now established its headquarters in the vicinities of Jenin and the different battalions together with their technical or medical groups are there.

Our squadron has arrived here one week ago; our camp is at approximately two miles north of Nazareth, not far from the small Arab village of Sauriya - a hiding place for bandits, according to some.

The landscape is nice and relaxing here. Plains and hills are all dressed up in a tender green interwoven by innumerable wild flowers. Here and there, some tiny gardens of olive trees, planted neatly behind their walls of dry stones; or some fir trees hanging on to the rocks on the hilltops. And then there are the almond trees, the prune trees, apple trees, dressed in their pink or white robes in order to celebrate spring's arrival.

A hill in the south separates from Nazareth. Nazareth, a name that we have learnt to pronounce ever since we have learnt that there is a God, what is it nowadays? A small town where houses of whitish stone agglomerate, dominated here and there by the tall walls and the red tile roofs of some monastery, topped by the police fortress, a huge modern building, as can be seen everywhere in Palestine. And all around, the green hills where cows and sheep feed, under the watch of little Arabs whose tattered clothes do not succeed in hiding the purity of their traits.

But besides all this, Nazareth is nowadays a town of soldiers: the largest monastery will be occupied by a hospital, there is an officers' club, a NNAFI, a cinema, a 'town major'. Soon our brigade's headquarters will be there. What a sad irony! The place chosen by Our Lord to live, now serving as dwelling place for soldiers, troops, whose mission in this war is among the most dangerous ones.

Ramat David, 10 April 1943

For three days now I have started my initial course on parachuting, this will give me an opportunity to qualify, which I was eagerly looking for. I am for a few days with the 10th battalion of 'Parachute Regiment', ten miles from Haifa.

For the time being, my training has consisted of gymnastic, physical culture and different exercises only, but this during six hours daily.

This training seemed to me almost too simple at first, but I have now changed my mind: the muscle soreness and the fatigue are beginning to defeat my physical resistance. Up till now I have not been preoccupied by the thought of the 'jumps', I will have to do as from next week. I think that it is due in a large extent to the instructors who are all excellent and also very reassuring.

Fear will start probably when I shall be aboard the plane.

12 April 1943

I have now finished my period of intensive physical culture in order to pass on to what is called 'the synthetic training': this will consist of different exercises of virtual sensations that are felt while descending by parachute.

I shall probably do my first jump on Thursday- weather permitting. Unfortunately rain has started, that rain which I have so often seen since October, and which I thought would end by the month of March. Today there have even been two or three hail storms; this bad weather renders life here even more unpleasant. I say 'even more' for I do not like the battalion mess at all! There is nothing but a large room, sad and bare, the food is poor - since my arrival there has not been a single day without beetroots! And we are only a few students, somewhat lost among the permanent members of the mess.

The 10th Battalion - which, with the 156th, plus a medical unit, plus a unit of the department of transmissions and our squadron, form the 4th Parachute Brigade for the time being, - was a battalion of the Royal Sussex, scarcely a few months ago. Now it has become a mix of different army regiments: Hussars, regiments of the guard, regiments of the British Counties, Yeomanry, regiment of tanks, Highlanders, all crowded here together in a messy way. And for the time being everybody holds on to their badges and colors, for the 'Parachute Regiment' has not yet any motto or coat of arms.

Nazareth was thus the point of reference for his new formation, his port of call. Christianity's Holy Place where one meditates on the coming of God in our flesh, in our history.

The site where the Gospel recounts the Announcement of the angel to Mary was now a locality where the announcement of the disembarking in Europe was being long expected. The place of the Holy Family's hidden life was now a hiding place for the preparation of the Allies' victory.

Hyacinthe had always dreamt of boarding an airplane. He would never have imagined that this first flight would take place in the sky of Nazareth, the place where the skies tore open for God to come down to live among men! This first flight was above an exceptional place on planet earth, chosen by God to pitch his Tent among us! On experiencing aerial sensations, Hyacinthe also discovered an exceptional panorama, a region of the world that had attracted pilgrims for centuries, without granting them the celestial view that he was now going to contemplate.

14 April 1943

Yesterday I had my first flight, a promenade of a few minutes in a Hudson, a bombing aeroplane converted into a transport for parachutists.

Funny how objects appear under different aspects when seen from above: rectangular fields whose colors are of different tones of greens, plantations of fir trees that are all symmetrical, Jewish colonies looking like toys, little streams that wind their ways and twist in a thousand convulsions. All that withdraws like a relief map, and it is with a childish joy that I looked out from one window to another.

Then I went in front of the wide open door, to see what would be my first feelings just before jumping.

I confess that I shuddered a little when measuring the distance that separated me from the ground, thinking that in a few days I would have to throw myself therein.

The bad weather is delaying the exercises a little, and it is probable that I will not do my first jump tomorrow. When the parachutes are wet, it takes several days for them to dry completely, and it seems that there are not enough for the amount of students.

It is one of those shortages that I cannot explain: since the war is costing the Empire hundreds of thousands of pounds sterling per day, why are we so often short of essential things while at the same time there is a waste of other articles?

21 April 1943

After many delays, the motherent I have been waiting for finally arrived yesterday: I did my first drop in parachute. I thought that I would return from this with an impression all different from what I am reporting now: I have found, in accomplishing such a deed, nothing but banality.

'A parachutist"! It is one of those words full of unknowns, the very mention of which contains all the emotion of a jump from the plane, of a fall into space, of a landing! But it is also one of those words that lose some of their prestige when they are felt for oneself, when the unknown has been replaced by a rather banal reality.

Yesterday morning therefore, at 6:00, I was at the aerodrome. Each one of us received a parachute and we started to try and adjust the harnesses, formed of very strong fabric bands, inside which we are tied and linked to the parachute that we shall carry in a bag on our back.

This first operation done, the sections ('sticks' as they are called) went one by one towards the starting track. Our turn came only at 8:30.

During all this time I tried to think of anything else but the drop from the plane: I have to say that I succeeded quite well: I had no apprehension, no nervousness. I was only annoyed by the endless time that we had to wait: one of the only two planes, which the R.A.F. could dispose of, had an engine problem and could not be used.

My annoyance grew into exasperation when towards 9:00 the announcement was made to us that one of the engines of the second

Hudson - the one that had served all morning - was not functioning too well and that we would have to come back at nine thirty. From 9:30 we were postponed to 11:00 and finally to 13:00.

I have to say that this waiting could not have a very good effect on the nerves: however it is with serenity and smiling - unless it was grimacing - that I embarked into the plane.

There, I started to go mentally over all that I had been taught: how to jump from the plane, how to turn in the air, how to land. And then, once more, I tried to joke with my companions rather than look too much towards the ground.

We had to jump in groups of three and I was the second in the first group. Here I should say that once in the air, the 'dispatcher' = a sergeant of the R.A.F. whose role is to tell the occupants of the plane at what time to jump - had tied our parachutes in such a way that they would open automatically. This is done by fixing a tape that one carries on the back to a similar one fixed to the body of the plane. When one jumps, the tension of the tape breaks the ropes that close the parachute bag and the latter opens automatically.

From reading this description, one could perhaps think that the entire system was not too solid; but a simple look on the large fabric bands that form the tapes and on the stainless steel attachments would be sufficient to convince sceptics. Besides, once one is thus attached, the instructor shows every one that he is solidly linked - this always has a considerable psychological effect - and he goes to take his place at the rear of the plane... on the seat of the W.C.! There has to be a comic side to all this, and our 'dispatcher', a great joker, never missed an opportunity to insist on this comical aspect.

A look on the landscape beneath and I understood that we were approaching our 'drop zone'. Indeed, the next motherent a red light appeared at the rear of the fuselage, near the door. It is the first signal and the instructor shouts "Action Stations, No, 1!"

The No 1 takes his position, hands on the sides of the opening, left foot on the threshold, ready to jump. Yet another second, and it is the green light. "Go!" yells the instructor and No 1 disappears out of the plane.

"Action stations, No 2! Go!" It's my turn! Here I am at the door, muscles tense: one more fraction of a second and I fall in the void. A fall of 20 or 30 feet before my parachute opens and I come to myself. I look at my parachute and I see that the lines are all entwined: I have to turn on myself a dozen times before regaining a normal position. It does not last long however, during this time I have taken a good position for landing, and I am satisfied to hear the instructor yell from the ground in his megaphone: *"You are coming down nicely, No 2!"*

It is from 1,000 feet that I have jumped and my drop lasts only one minute. Now I don't let my eyes wander off the ground. It is an impression of wellbeing that one feels while descending this way, comfortably attached to one's harness.

At the last moterent, the ground seems to come up towards me with a surprising rapidity: there is some wind and my body oscillates now with a pendulum movement. I touch ground with some violence and roll on my back before throwing myself on the side, as should be done.

Now, one should get away from the harness: the force of the wind renders this operation hard: I am dragged over a certain distance before being able to get out of it. Fortunately the ground is formed of soft soil with young shoots of wheat; if one is not afraid of getting dirty, there is no more fear.

I am quickly on my feet with only a little pain at the shoulder and at the neck, and ready to start again.

As best as I can, I fold up my parachute and carry it towards the truck: from there it will be transported to a shed where it will be cleaned and dried by experts for its next jump. And here is my first experience as a parachutist!

The coming of Jesus at Nazareth, his hidden life in Mary, and then in the Holy Family, marked the beginning of the Kingdom of God on earth. But during this year 1943 the earthly kingdom was in everybody's mind. By joining the squadron of parachutists, Hyacinthe had received from the Supreme Commandment a secret document that he glued to one of his notebooks.

SECRET
"You will soon be engaged in a great enterprise - the invasion of Europe. Our goal is to provoke, in partnership with our Allies, and

our comrades on other fronts, the total defeat of Germany. It is only by such a total victory that we shall be able to liberate ourselves as well as our countries from the fear and menace of the Nazi tyranny.

The next element of our mission is the liberation of those peoples of Western Europe who suffer presently under the German oppression.

Before engaging in this operation, I have a personal message addressed to you, and to your personal involvement, with regards to the inhabitants of Allied nations.

As representatives of your country, you will be welcome with a profound gratitude by the liberated peoples, who waited years for this deliverance. It is of the utmost importance that this sentiment of friendship and good reputation not be spoilt in any case by imprudent and mediocre attitudes on your part.

By a courteous and generous behaviour, you can on the contrary reinforce this sentiment.

The inhabitants of Nazi-occupied Europe have suffered great privations, and you will find that many of them lack even the strict minimum. You, on your part, have been and will continue to be supplied adequately in food, clothing and other necessities.

You must not exhaust the stocks of food and other supplies, already lean, by inconsiderate sales, as well as by favouring the black market, which would only increase the inhabitants' privations.

The rights of individuals, as much their person as their properties, have to be scrupulously respected, as in your own country. You have to remember, always, that these peoples are our friends and our Allies.

I recommend strongly to each one of you to keep continually in mind that by your actions, not only you, as individuals, but also your country, will be judged. By establishing a relationship with the liberated peoples, based on comprehension and mutual respect, we shall contribute to their unconditional assistance for the defeat of our common enemy. Thus, we shall place the foundations of a durable peace, without which our grand efforts will have been of no use."

Towards Liberation

Hyacinthe knew that from then on the goal was a landing in Europe. However, a long road had yet to be travelled before that day. More trials and surprises were going to await him on his meandering route to France.

19 May 1941

I am back from the canteen where I went to have a glass with the men: evening made of beers and singing to celebrate our departure. Yes, we leave tomorrow morning for a destination that I do not know yet, but I suspect it to be Tunisia.

With the conquest of the enemy's ultimate retrenchment in North Africa a new phase is starting for us: I am certain that next month or in July, we shall take part in an operation. I am leaving with a certain melancholy, due to the apprehension that maybe our days are now counted. Nevertheless I maintain my optimism: one should always persuade oneself that we will get through it safely.

As a parachutist he was constantly aware of the risk of war. He knew his vulnerability when, projected from the sky, his life relied upon a piece of fabric, exposed to the enemy, engaged in battle! This battle should have been in Italy. But destiny decided otherwise.

S.S. 'Ohna' (In the Mediterranean) - 26 May 1943

Yesterday it was the departure from Alexandria, perhaps the farewell to Egypt. Very early in the morning, we arrived on the quay and, little by little, the mass of men who got out of the big military trucks stepped into the ship, congested the corridors, filling the tween-decks, overflowing onto the decks.

Our squadron forms quite a small number among these troops. We are only about thirty men and four officers. But there are also some detachments from other units of the brigade: indeed, the brigade has been divided into four groups travelling aboard different ships – so as to avoid putting all the eggs in the same basket!

On board there are also some soldiers of the guard, some Basutos and Sudanese, not to mention the small groups of other units. Those Sudanese with their scars on the cheeks are superb: they seem to have been sculpted out of ebony.

We always travel incognito - within the limits of the possible: no eagles on the sleeve, the special casks at the bottom of the trunks and the word 'parachute' banished from all conversation: our squadron itself is nothing but the '4th Squ' for the moterent. Officially, we don't know anything about our destination: I learnt however that the ship would berth first at Tripoli and that we ourselves would be disembarked some place in Tunisia.

28 May 1943

Third birthday spent away from mine, away from the country! On such days, dates with which certain memories are associated, I feel a little sadder, solitude seems to weigh a little heavier. And then, how avoid some bitterness when I think of the way in which I spend these years of my youth, to say the least!

I know well that one is still young at forty, or even forty-five. But when one is thirty, does not one lose that spontaneity, a lot of those illusions also, which add such charm to existence?

True, it is only my twenty-seventh birthday today. But alas! I know well that these few years of war have made me force the pace, have brought me beyond the limit of a real youth!

The four ships of our convoy continue to advance towards the west, under the protection of the destroyers, which have been so justly compared to watchdogs watching over a herd.

This afternoon we have lost sight of the land that lay alongside since yesterday. We have passed Tobrouk, Derma, agglomerations of constructions that one hardly distinguished. Now we are in the Syrian gulf. Till now no alert: the Mediterranean seems all ours. But today this Mediterranean is a little rough: I feel that if this continues, things will go bad.

Things had started to move. Hyacinthe was preparing himself for a definitive step, for the final assault for which he had been prepared all along! But the waiting time was sometimes long and trying!

13 June 1943

A quite sad Sunday today: a Sunday spent for the most part by sitting outside my tent in front of a transmitter-receiver radio set. The dust, the breeze, the dried grass, the cactus!

Where are the filaos and the green grass of Mauritius?

The desert of his soul was not always irrigated, and the true combat was psychological. These thoughts had to be fought relentlessly, in order not to be dragged by them into those dangerous nostalgic ways. Then came a physical trial to which he had not been prepared at all, and which added even more pressure to his spirits.

I make a descent in parachute with the 156th battalion, to take part in manoeuvres as a referee. The excellent landing that I perform restores my confidence, somewhat disturbed after my last but one jump near the lake of Galilee.

Unfortunately, the long march of that morning awakens a pain at the heel, which had started some time before. The result of the doctor's auscultation, whom I consult this morning, is not satisfying at all. He considers that I should rest a month or two, or completely forget about my career as a parachutist.

Upon his advice, I have to see a specialist tomorrow morning. What a catastrophe if I had to really give up this career that I have chosen in a sense of sacrifice but which is now so dear to my heart. Actually, I just received those letters that I was awaiting with such anxiety: the first impressions of Mother and Eda since I joined the squadron. As I expected, they give me their approval: but how not to be moved by the resignation appearing between the lines!

Now the die is cast: the specialist's decision has only confirmed my fears. On 10 July, at the same time that the attack against Sicilia was being launched, attack to which took part certain troops of my division, I had to accept that, for medical reasons, I was not fit enough to perform my present duties.

The specialist must have read the expression of disappointment on my face when he rendered this verdict, for he added: *"I am awfully sorry, but I am afraid I can't help it!"*

I therefore have to abandon my career as a parachutist: gone are the drops from airplanes, the walks, the exercises, although difficult, but that I appreciated nevertheless; finished above all is the hope of taking an active part in any operation.

What shall I do now, I don't know yet. Hardiman has suggested to me to stay in the squadron where I would have a role in the administration as 'non-jumping member', but the idea does not please me at all. Such a post does not even exist, and, if it was created, I don't see how it could enter into the frame of the present organization; and then, I like the squadron especially for the active life that I have there – or rather, that I had there.

It would not be the same if I were to become a bureaucrat (a pen-pusher or office employee). But aren't those the only positions that I can hold now, those of bureaucrats? Whatever I do, it is probably an old man job that I should expect, quite a cushy one where I would not be tired! While waiting for a decision to be taken about me, it seems to me that I have become useless in my uniform, a good-for-nothing for the army.

This additional trial consumed him interiorly, and the coming summer did not improve things:

2 August 1943

I have to force myself to come and write these notes: it is a true effort that I have to make to take my pen: whether the heat, the nervousness, the atmosphere, all seem to stop me.

Now that it has been decided that I shall stay in the squadron as 'reinforcement officer' until I can occupy other functions in two or three months, I have to try to get used to the idleness that drains me of all energy. Besides, how can one feel any energy when the heat hits sometimes 50 degrees in the shade and when the dust thickens day by day?

And now the supply of water has been reduced to one gallon per person daily.

I have reasons to believe that soon we shall not be here anymore - without knowing nevertheless where we shall be. At this motherent minds are tending towards the idea of a future operation for our brigade: but nobody knows anything anyway.

10 August 1943

Today the sirocco blows, as a supplement to the heat, raising the dust that seems to take this opportunity to become more familiar. And, as always, the flies are here, to complete the picture.

For the present time, I start fortunately to defeat my idleness: I have new occupations that keep me busy enough. I am actually in charge of the squadron's vehicles: this has allowed the major to grant my request to take part in the future operation. Indeed, I should accompany the squadron with a few jeeps, transported in gliders. That means that I, myself, shall go in one of those aircrafts.

I confess that I agree to this solely because, for the motherent, it is the only way for me to engage into action. In fact few people are conscious that the role played by troops transported in gliders is much more dangerous than that of the parachutists: On the invasion of Sicily the victims have testified this. One feels so defenceless when, instead of having a parachute on the back, one is strapped to the seat by a belt! But, *"A Dieu Vat!"* (It is up to God's grace!)

Tizi N'Kouilal - Algeria - 5 September 1943

It has been a week now that we have left the dusty camp of M'Saken, its cactus and its olive trees, to come to Algeria, this Algeria that I wanted so much to know.

A long trip covering a thousand kilometres through towns and mountains, arid plains and shady forests. We spend the first night at Tunis, and then, take the road to Medjez, Souk-ek-Arba; the winding roads in the mountain, the tall trees, the chalet-resort *'des Chênes'*, and then the border: we are in Algeria.

La Calle, a small old-style port where old sailors wearing caps and thick mustachios, exchanging few words, smoke the pipe on the quay. And then at all speed - I am in a jeep with two officers and a chauffeur - we go towards Bone where we arrive at nightfall.

Bone, industrial port with its big phosphates warehouses, its large paved roads, its beautiful Byzantine basilica on top of the hill, its boulevard where the coffee tables huddle together, Bone has nothing interesting to offer for the passing visitor.

After spending the night there, we leave for Constantine. First of all it is a coastal road, and then at Jemmapes, we turn towards the South.

Twisty roads on and on, and hills on and on, along this beautiful road sometimes all white with brightness across harvested fields, and sometimes all fresh and shady. The road grows steeper, the turns more impressive.

Another bend and here is Constantine on the horizon. A rock with vertical and bare surfaces, crowned with light-coloured gigantic buildings, a suspension bridge which links the city to another rock far up there, surmounted by a winged statue, a fairy-like landscape, a surreal city in an imaginary world, this is the city which bears the name of a Roman Emperor.

Little by little, we climb up the road, which just manages to hang on to the cliff-side, then goes right through the rock, and with great effort hauls itself to the top.

And up there, it is not a small village that we reach, nor a gathering of strange and picturesque constructions but for sure a large modern city: superb twelve-storey buildings, grand casino, huge industrial buildings, linked together or divided by a series of stairs and narrow and steep streets.

A day and two nights at Constantine, and then again the main road, the restful landscape is ever changing.

At Beni Mansour we turn towards Maillot and then it is a picturesque and frightful mountain track that takes us at last to the alpine refuge of Tizi N'Kouilal, in the mountain range of Djurdjura. In the mountains all around: there are fir trees, but mostly glazes and a little dried grass, a good training ground for the troops.

The day following my arrival I go to Alger, a journey of five hours that takes us across numerous villages bearing French or Arab names, villages where the small church with the bell-tower surmounted by an enormous nest of storks is always in display.

And now here is Alger: a big harbour full of war ships and trade buildings, suburbs with plenty of enormous industrial buildings, superb modern ones – such as the general government offices- bordering with the inevitable 'rococo' structures, shops with facades designs worthy of the best French artists, the Allied G.Q.G Centre in North Africa, the actual capital of the French Empire.

And now I have to put aside pencil and notebook: an urgent message just arrived to inform us that we have to go back immediately to M'Saken.

Is my tourist promenade going to change abruptly into a less pleasant outing in enemy territory? It won't be long before I am informed.

M'Saken - 18 September 1943

The following day after I wrote those last lines, we left towards our camp at all speed, travelling 26 hours with only brief stops for meals.

We still did not know why we had to come back in haste: personally I thought that the division was going to settle in Sicily in order to be closer to Italy where the operations were starting. But, hardly had we arrived here when we learnt that we had to prepare ourselves to take part in an immediate operation.

General turmoil pervades in the camp where everyone assembles his belongings hastily so as to leave the very same evening. As for me, the major announced what I had half expected: I could not leave with the squadron - my role was to join the troop later with a handful of men and heavy luggage.

I tried my best to convince Hardiman to let me leave immediately, but it was of no avail: the medical state in which I am presently made that impossible.

I therefore left that night for Bizerte to see the troops embark and to bring back to camp whatever they would not be able to take onboard.

When I shall read these lines all over one day - if ever this happens - I shall perhaps ask myself the reason for this enthusiasm, this crazy desire to be involved in battle, rather than a regret for not being able to participate. Such a question will remain without an answer if then I cannot remember what one feels when seeing one's fellows *en route* for the front, while for one's part having to stay safely behind.

Yes, now they are all gone: red berets, machineguns, equipment, all rushed into the cruisers, *en route* for the bloody adventure.

I said: they went aboard the cruisers. There is a shortage of transport aircrafts at the motherent - that is why the division had to go by sea instead of taking the air route. And now that I am back here, the news from there reaches me daily. They have landed at Taranto, without opposition - the Italian armistice having just been officially announced. Afterwards, they have advanced towards the north, the 4th brigade of the *avant-garde*.

Three days ago, the victims numbered the following: 14 killed, 14 wounded and 20 missing. Most of them of the 156th, the one I should have joined.

Our General is the first one to be hurt, and dies two days after. The very day of embarking, I saw him on the quay, full of beans, keeping an eye on everything. He was, as was to be expected, at the head of *avant-garde patrols*, when a burst of machinegun hit him at the head.

Of the squadron I know nothing at all yet. How many of my comrades are lying forever on Italian soil?

This situation awakened in him feelings that he could not handle. Hyacinthe was now at the end of his rope. On 21 September, he wrote:

But when are we going to leave these olive-trees and this dust? They are growing more and more hateful to me. I feel that I am becoming more and more listless everyday; I have no energy, I have no desire to do anything, everything seems indifferent to me.

Mauritius has turned into a distant world for me, whose news I read within long intervals. And how can I express how much it means to me, this little country, especially those who are there, those who wait for me there, who pray for me?

But the day will come...

29 October 1943

The future looks somewhat better now: the day before yesterday, it has been more or less decided that I'll soon go to Italy to take some troops of the brigade there.

I shall have to come back perhaps, but I hope to be able to make arrangement for someone else to be sent back in my place. I still don't know what the division is doing there; is it in Italy for quite a long time, or will it be sent to another operational theatre? Nobody here seems to know.

9 November in the morning, departure for Bizerte with about twenty trucks - we reach there under the rain: everywhere is but mud and enormous water puddles, sticky mud ploughed and kneaded by the incessant flow of numerous British and American vehicles.

We wait all afternoon near the aerodrome all littered with debris of French hydroplanes, old biplanes whose antique structures look strangely out-fashioned to our eyes used to modern planes.

And then it is the 'Texas Transit Camp' during a week, that horrible hillside camp where one sinks ankle-deep in the slippery mud, a place where no effort is made to provide the occupants with the slightest comfort.

Tents with muddy grounds, rain leaking through the sides, mess composed of a large tent where a few tables and benches are just thrown together, where one eats in one's own utensil that one washes, a total lack of water for one's own toilet needs, taps that I have never seen anywhere else, one could accept all that with a great heart - one would even say that it was luxury - if one was near the front line. But at Bizerte it would be so easy to do better!

And during this delicious stay, counter-orders succeeded with utmost speed to orders about our departure for Italy

On the 14th, I managed finally to embark the luggage and a few men in three different landing crafts, and, after seeing their big front doors close on the vehicles, material and luggage of all sorts, I had to come back to Sousse with a few men, all disappointed for not having been able to leave. But once back at the camp, and once my report made to major Powell, he told me that I had to go immediately to Italy by plane and return to North Africa once my mission completed.

A few quick bites, a swipe of shaving, and I jump in the jeep *en route* for Tunis. I spend a day there and on the 17th in the morning I embark in a D.C.3 at Al Aovina Airport.

It is a pleasant sensation to see the large door of the D.C.3 close before take-off - when I will pass through this door again to disembark from the plane, it will be at ground level again, and not at 1,000 feet in altitude!

And so we leave the coasts of North Africa - soon the belt of land recedes behind us. Nothing but the great blue immensity beneath - or the tangled extension of big clouds, grey and white, that become vaporous and immaterial as soon as we get through – then we look like a group of human beings lost in a universe of magicians and fairies. But are we not rather in the kingdom of gremlins, those little men who war relentlessly against aviators and parachutists?

A flight of one hour and a quarter, and we are above Sicily - for one quarter of an hour we fly over fields and valleys, hills and villages, and then it is Palermo. We hover once above the aerodrome and then we land.

A stop of one hour - a few passengers go down, others come up and we leave again.

A flight of one hour above Sicily and now it is Catania where we stop for lunch - lunch at the American mess where we eat pineapples with juice, meat and mashed potatoes together in one dish.

The plane takes off and once again we fly over the sea for a little more than one hour until the coasts of Italy appear in the vicinities of Taranto. Opposite me in the airplane is the General Crerar, commandant of the Canadian army corps.

This time I get my luggage out of the plane - I must not go further. At this aerodrome - which is about fifteen kilometres to the north-east of the town of Taranto - the damages caused by our bombardments are still to be seen, similarly to those in Sicily: most of corrugated iron sheets stripped from the aircraft hangars, enemy planes in pieces, some bomb craters not yet filled. But here like elsewhere, endless back and forth motions of British and American aircraft: there is not a single minute without one taking off or landing – bomber planes, fighters, transport aircrafts.

At last am I here, in Italy! Just a few weeks ago I seriously thought that I would never be there, in the country of Victor-Emmanuel!

Now, all that's left for me to do is to find a truck that will agree to take me to Taranto, where I hope to find the squadron one way or another.

There happens to be a truck going to town - I am now on the tarred road, all shiny with rain, between the trees that have worn their autumnal outfit, the beautiful espalier vines, the olive trees always green around which the farm-women gather for the harvest.

I am entering Taranto now, quite a big town with a rather banal and sad appearance. I see no damaged buildings - it is mainly in the port region and railway tracks that considerable damages have been caused.

Civilian life seems to continue without considerable changes: at the 'officers' club, where I leave my luggage, I am surprised to see a beautiful hall with luxurious decors, where smart waiters in jackets serve tea and cakes such as I have not seen since I left Egypt.

The Italian Navy is everywhere - thousands of sailors and officers pack the streets and do not seem to be much preoccupied by the war.

What will shock me even more upon my return is to see at the aerodrome of Bari some Italian aviators near their planes on which a green, white and red flag has replaced the three beam weapons of the fascist party.

How can we fail to understand and share the opinion of the French people who cannot get used to the idea that the Italians are now our cobelligerents?

But let us leave politics alone and go back to Taranto.

By sheer coincidence, I meet some officers of the squadron, all surprised to see me in Italy, and I go immediately to the docks for the discharge of landing crafts that I had seen leave Bizerte with our luggage and which were arriving now.

An air raid alert rushes out towards the shelters, in quite a disarray, the Italian soldiers working on the port, while we continue our task in the bitter air of a screen of smoke immediately established to protect the ships.

I am off with the luggage to the brigade headquarters at Gioia del Colle, which is about forty kilometres to the north.

The stay in Italy was short lived.

And so, on the 17th in the morning, we would see Sousse for the last time - the bell tower of Saint Felix, the Kasbah walls, the French caserns, all these buildings destroyed and hurt by the bombs, all fading out, passing from a world of reality to a world of memories.

Our North African phase was coming to an end. En route for England! Yes, this is our destination. For months, the rumour had been whispered by and large, one of those "informal news from reliable source" transmitted by word of mouth, then, after amplification, the information was confirmed: *"The Airborne Div. is going Back home!"*

We have been sworn to secrecy, the chatterboxes have been threatened of all sorts of sanctions and finally the clothes and special casks have been set aside in bags, soon followed by the red berets and the blue wings. Once more we were becoming an anonymous troop wearing varied badges.

And now, we're aboard the train, going towards Alger.

A bad third-class compartment that I share with 'Doc' Brown – unspeakable mess, humidity everywhere, floors littered with papers, cigarette stubs, food leftovers, greasy clothes coated with soot. We have to live amongst that for three days. We eat when the train stops - we don't know when the stops will occur, nor how long they will last - already we are more than 12 hours behind schedule.

Yesterday, one of our sergeants, thinking that the train had stopped for some time, has had to jump onto the wagon that was leaving and, as he slipped on the step, his leg was severed.

Everything takes place in a French style, in a family way: at every station the train controller chats with the station chief, and the information that he communicates to us after these exchanges are never exact: we will soon have French chauffeurs, sometimes American ones or English ones; for some part of the journey we will have an American loco, which will soon be replaced by an electric or steam French loco!

And the cold grows more and more unbearable. Already we see the mountains peaks covered with white snow, in the neighbourhood of Alger.

Good things come to those who wait!

H.M. J. Maloja - In the Mediterranean - 27 December 1943

We embarked on the 25th in the evening - or rather the 26th at 4:00. Christmas Eve I spent at Blida - dinner at the Allied officers' circle, dreadfully banal, and then midnight mass at the town's church.

Thank God we've had that Christmas Mass - wherever we attend, whatever the environment, it is always the celebration that commemorates the birth of the Saviour, the Sacrifice enlightened by an even greater mysticism on this sacred anniversary. It is also a motherent when thoughts get nearer to those one loves, for the soul feels better suited for prayer then. For me, this Christmas has not only been the third one far from my own people, but this time not the smallest rejoicing, however poor, has marked the occasion. It is perhaps better this way.

So, on the 25th I arrived in Alger in the rain and the wind to embark on the Maloja, big ship of 21 000 tons of P.L.O line, and on the 26th in the evening, we said goodbye to the African land.

Now we sail in convoy towards the west, eleven large light grey shells, filled with troops, with their escort of cruisers and destroyers. On board we are about 4,000 soldiers and 500 officers – on top of each other everywhere.

31 December 1943

Last day of the year! The day when I feel overcome by a deeper sadness, the time when the absence of the one I love is even more strongly felt. From this cabin, on board the ship that sways and rolls in the Atlantic, it is towards Mauritius that my thoughts go, towards the place where I would like to be.

But it is above all hopelessness that I feel when I think of those three years which have just passed, or of a future where nothing good seems to await me – at the present time, at least. Years of my youth spent in uniform, doing a job that I don't like, in an atmosphere and a surrounding always foreign: not even the satisfaction to say to myself that I have been in the front line, where true soldiers are, since I have always remained in the rear or on communication lines.

And the future too, I look at it with no courage: war will end in 1944, I am certain; but, if I have been spared from death till then, I shall have to face civilian life on my return, going back to my work which I have but imperfectly mastered, and that I have now completely forgotten: no, I should rather think of others, of those whose home has been destroyed, whose family does not exist anymore: I should think of Mother, Eda, the family, the country.

Isn't that enough to bring me the strength and optimism that threaten to forsake me? If I feel jaded, discouraged, full of bitterness, I have only myself to blame.

Here am I, in England. 1944 has entered the scene - a January 1st, quite commonplace, with no festivity to brighten up.

Our journey has thus continued, under a permanent grey sky and by a sea that became more and more rough, until the 4th in the morning. It is then the arrival into the Mersey estuary, the river through which the ship proceeds up amidst the busy tugs.

And now, it is Liverpool, its countless chimneys whose smoke blackens the already-grey sky, its buildings of blackened bricks, the workers housing estates, dominated here and there by a steeple, or the tower of a large building.

The ship docks at the quay, everybody is on the ship decks. For everyone it is "home", that magic word which fills every mouth - for everybody but not for me, because England, even if I am happy to come there, is for me but another stage.

A military orchestra greets us on the quays by playing English popular tunes. And then it is the Navy or Army superior officers who welcome us too.

In a short time, Hyacinthe's squadron hit the road.

Now, it's the English countryside that is passing by: the undulating meadows, the fences, the hedges, the clumps of trees, all winter bare; the big workhorses, all is there: reality looks like a scenery. And I forgot the small brick or stone cottages greened by age, with their slated or thatched roofs. Everything has the charm of past times, but a past time associated with a meticulous cleanliness, a perfect order.

From 4 January 1944, day of his arrival in England, Hyacinthe's notes were increasingly scarce. His mission was becoming more and more precise.

These days I leave for Scotland. I have been affected to S.A.S. for one week and at the end of that period, it will be decided if I shall be transferred definitely.

All in God's hand now!

As a matter of fact, he was accepted and remained with this group. He described the atmosphere a little bit:

Days pass: with the return of the sun and the apparition of the first buds, one starts to count the days which separate us from the invasion of the continent, that invasion which 'Monty' does not want us to call the second front.

Nothing is known about it except that it will take place: but if neither the man on the street nor myself know any official information, every one has his own opinion, his ideas. Shall I be part of those troops, shall I be among the first wave to land in Europe? It is my wish.

In the regiment, the training continues, intensifies. I hope that I shall 'keep it up'. I fear for my foot and my knees, which are not too strong.

Yesterday I returned from exercises which have lasted two days and two nights - forty-three hours without sleep, during which we run about twenty-five miles, sometimes under a striking rain and through swamps where one risks to sink at every step. Once back, how good it is to find a hot bath and a bed!

Since yesterday, one would not believe it's spring. The weather is grey and windy as in winter. After our last week exercise, we're getting ready to do another one, a little shorter, these days.

As on the eve of the invasion of Italy, I wait with as much impatience as all those around me, that the events become clearer. In veiled terms, everyone has an opinion, whispers the last 'information from reliable source', speaks of the squadrons that will be leaving first and those which will have to wait; only those who know say nothing.

We're a good group in the 'D' Squadron to which I am attached. First there's Ian Fenwick, our Commander, the artist whose humorous drawings are known by all... Many times, he reminds me of Max. And then there's Pat Garstin, our Captain, a tall Irish who took part in the first campaign of France as well as those of Tunisia and Sicily; Bill Anderson, a guy so nice despite his gruff looks, who fought in Spain during the Revolution, and then again in France, Tunisia, and Sicily.

My roommates are two Scots, 'Sock' Riding and Jimmy Watson, two intimate friends who both come from the Highland Light Infantry; and then there are three sub-lieutenants, a little young and lacking in experience but good comrades nevertheless.

During his leaves, he got acquainted with his cousins Souchon who lived in England.

These family-immersions rekindled a tremendous, too deeply buried, happiness, and brought him a consolation he would not have found anywhere else.

I have gone on leave. The whole regiment was absent for thirteen days and willy-nilly I had to do the same. I cannot complain however - although I am starting to find that I hardly do any work for the salary I receive - seven weeks of perm in three months, it's unbelievable! I tell myself however that soon things will get tough, and that we shall have to pay dearly for this current period of near-freedom. When I think of it cold-headedly, I am willing to agree that we of the S.A.S. shall not be that numerous to come back from the operations accompanying the invasion of the continent. But I try not to dwell too heavily on the subject.

For the last three days, I have been at Marie's in Leatherhead. Quiet Easter day in the countryside where spring clothes every tree branch with a tender green garment. The sun dares not come outright, and there're still some cold days in this beginning of April.

Yesterday we were at Laure Doble's, in Sussex. She lives in a small and very ancient house, very old with that true oldness with its low ceilings, its all-exposed beams, old pieces of oak all greened by time. There, I find the Mauritian hospitality: Laure, whom I did not know, speaks of her friendship with her cousins - my Mother and my aunts.

Here it's Marie's kindness and attentions that constantly remind me that the family, this institution to which we are so attached in Mauritius, is a priceless thing, and one of the most beautiful given to us.

That priceless institution! It had left neither his thoughts, nor his heart, nor his guts... He felt that he belonged to his family as light belongs to the sun, as heat belongs to fire.

Hyacinthe dreamt of founding his own family with Eda, of having numerous children and of bringing them up in love and faith, in the peaceful atmosphere of his native Mauritius.

These dreams cropped up again at his cousins Souchon's, and more than ever he thought of what would be his life with Eda.

He pictured their house, which he enjoyed conceiving in his mind, their future garden, and above all everything that he would like to transmit to his children.

He could still nourish his dreams before H hour, before throwing himself body and soul into the fray.

The H hour! He dreaded that motherent and sometimes wondered if he would have sufficient courage to dig up the war hatchet, to fight at the risk of his life.

After a chopped itinerary, fractioned in different stages, interspersed with surprises, there remained one obvious fact: the crucial motherent was approaching, and many of them would stay on the battlefield.

Now I close this notebook probably for a long time When I shall come back to write some hasty notes, I shall be in a camp waiting for my departure for France, in occupied country, far behind the enemy lines perhaps.

Or are these notes that I write now the last ones?

Touché!

La Ferté-Alais is a village of the French countryside where war was highly experienced, and for a long time. Many men from the French Resistance had constituted an official network, and worked secretly in collaboration with *maquisards* (Resistance fighters) and the *Réfractaires au Service du Travail Obligatoire* (S.T.O.) (Obligatory Labour services).

The woods of the region offered an ideal framework to live in hiding at tens of kilometres away from Paris. Drops had regularly been performed in the higher areas of the village, on the plateau of Tertre on the border of the Bois du Gland. Through this, several tons of material had been recuperated and henceforth re-expedited.

However, before this 4 July 1944 certain alarming signs had been noticed. Indeed, some inhabitants of the borough had rather chosen collaboration with the Germans. Anomalies appeared in the operation, and all that alarmed the team, which remained on their guard.

End of June, a man of the region went to Paris in the hope of reselling some parachutes that had been found in the edge of the forest. However, the Gestapo had intercepted the reseller and had him confess under torture that drop-offs had occurred regularly near La Ferté-Alais.

On the 3rd July, the BBC had broadcasted a message to the team of La Ferté-Alais:

"Its song tells me everything" ("son chant me dit tout") that announced the imminent coming of a drop off. The Resistance knew that this was at risk, but it was hard for them to evaluate its significance because suspicions of denunciation had not been solidly

confirmed. They waited long without noticing anything unusual. However, because of the weather forecast, too bad in England, the plane did not take off. The next day, on 4 July, the same message was repeated twice, which indicated the coming of the parachutists.

The plane approached in the ink-black night. From high, the silhouette of the sleeping world looked like a model made of paper and cardboard.

Last verifications, last prayers, before the last jump. In that semi-darkness which extended as wide as an ocean, a few pale lights appeared here and there. Hyacinthe then dreamt about those houses, those homes, little islets where life and love still existed and resisted always.

The twelve young parachutists did not talk, or very little. It was cold in those planes, hanging between sky and ground. They were embarked on a perilous mission: one month stay on French soil, to sabotage the airports of the west of Paris, in Ile-de-France.

One more plane had crossed the Channel to achieve its objective. One of those thousands little targets to aim, so as to attain victory over the Nazis.

"Pray for us, now and at the hour of our death", Hyacinthe put his hand to his pocket and felt the rosary he was taking with him. He trusted it as a weapon against fear and discouragement, as a banner held against the surrounding threats

While the plane approached the zone, the *Résistants* ran in the middle of the night towards the *Bois de Bouray*. It was about two o'clock in the morning. Suddenly, a shot tore the silence of the night and one man fell.

Panic-stricken, the others fled as fast as their legs could run except one, more daring, who chose rather to hide in order to understand what was happening. The Germans had been notified and they had come in great numbers for an ambush.

While the nocturnal silence reclaimed its rights, at a few hundreds of metres above their heads twelve young men jumped one after another. The plane did a u-turn thereon, abandoning them to their sad fate.

The Germans, who were scrutinizing the sky, saw the dances of a few parachutes that could be detected owing to the clear night. Hidden in the thickets or behind trees, the Nazis were waiting patiently for their preys unaware of the awful trap that had been laid out for them.

One by one, they landed, rolling on the soil, while letting the weight of their body terminate the braking action of the parachutes. But without warning, the machine-gun burst out, and panic seized the hearts of the S.A.S. youths.

Some of them managed to escape into the woods, but were caught up by the Germans who had anticipated everything, including this scenario.

During the chase, which lasted till dawn, another Résistant armed with grenades arrived to avenge his friends. Alas! He was hurt by the enemy shots and found near dead later. Three of the parachutists managed to escape, and the others were trapped like mice.

Hyacinthe lay on the ground. Hurt by the German shots, he could not get up. Surely he had felt the impact shock of the bullets, but he did not yet suffer from his wounds. He managed to get out of his harness and felt a hot liquid trickling on his hand: it was his blood flowing abundantly. He palpated his body and felt worse and worse. Blood did not frighten him. But he felt imprisoned in that body that he could not control anymore. "My God! I am hurt!" he thought.

Immediately after being captured, he was transported into a truck where he was stretched down. Bending his head, he recognized some of his companions whose silhouettes came out against the morning mist. In vain he tried to see if all of them were there and alive.

His suffering was increasing and at times he was even forced to curl up in an attempt to reduce it.

He felt the flux of his spurting blood, and his body grieved all over. His wounds could be localized: one at the shoulder blade, one at the thigh, and the one that burnt most, at the bottom of his back. He knew that he had just escaped death, and inwardly thought: *"I'm alive! As long as there's life, there's hope!"*

The sun was starting to extend its rays over this plain where thousands of dew droplets shone like crystals. With his closed eyes, tears of pain were also shining. He heard the Germans, more and more numerous around the truck where he lay.

One of his companions succeeded in negotiating with the enemy for the authorisation to give a morphine shot to Hyacinthe. They exchanged a few words, and three other wounded were led to his side. He recognized his companions: one who suffered like him, his uniform stained with blood, another already unconscious, maybe dead. Corpses were buried in a field, then the noise of doors being slammed shut was heard, and the procession of trucks started on its journey.

The morphine allayed his pain a little, but the vehicles ran on chaotic roads, causing jolts that rendered the journey highly uncomfortable. The trucks finally connected with the departmental route and took the direction of the capital.

Paris was well awake on this 5th July, even if it was still suffering under the enemy's yoke. The roads were deserted, and the trucks arrived at La Pitié-Salpêtrière hospital, which had been requisitioned years ago to be turned into a German military hospital.

When the nurses came close to examine the wounded, he could read in their eyes some signs of compassion. One of them was already dead and was removed first. The three others were placed on stretchers and disappeared behind the doors of the building.

Those who were not grievously wounded were led to the 16th arrondissement of the city, at 3 bis place des Etats-Unis. The building had been requisitioned since 1940, when the owner had fled to New York. It was quite a simple Parisian building, without any particularity but occupied by the Germans, which had turned it into a prison.

Scarcely arrived, Hyacinthe's fellow prisoners started to undergo severe interrogatories, which afterwards turned into torture sessions.

The security police of the territory (or 'Gestapo' - Geheime Staats Polizei) plunged them one by one in a burning hot water tub then into an icy one, whilst immersing their head violently with threats of drowning them. Those who resisted this first trial were then submitted to nail pulling with a big pair of pliers. Their Calvary was only beginning!

At La Pitié-Salpêtrière, Hyacinthe was tortured too. They were determined to make him speak by all means, but the worst torture that he had to bear physically was the lack of medical care. Indeed, the wound at the bottom of his back was serious and getting infected. He twisted with pain but no one took any notice of him, as priority was given to the Germans.

One of the soldiers who were watching over him showed some compassion. He was a young Austrian who, while sorting Hyacinthe's personal belongings, had seen a rosary stuck in his pant pocket. He took it and handed it back to him. Everything had been taken away from him: he could only keep this rosary once placed on the Rock of Agony and the Stone of Golgotha.

He clutched this priceless treasure very tightly.

The hours passed slowly. He had lost everything. He no longer possessed anything. But his heart was still beating, life circulated in his weakened body, and this rosary gave him a tremendous courage. He felt linked by this prayer to his dear ones who had received no news of him and who were starting to worry. He would have liked to write just a few words, just to tell his love to his closest ones, to appease his mother, his dear fiancée, his brothers and sisters. But it was impossible since first of all he had no strength. And most of all he was indeed a prisoner.

He had lost everything but the hope to see them again. And he prayed as fervently as he could, whilst passing, through his poor awakened fingers, one wooden rosary bead to the next. This unique treasury was like an umbilical cord linking him to all his loved ones.

Sometimes he dozed in a state of semi-coma; sometimes he twisted with pain and tried desperately to find a more comfortable posture to attenuate his torment.

It often occurred to him to think about his fellow-prisoners: where were they? What were they enduring? He imagined them in Germany and it was only much later that he learnt about their sad itinerary.

He also thought of those he had left in England, wondering how they were reacting to this news of their capture. He thought of the allied soldiers, progressing, and he begged Heaven to help them to reach Paris to liberate the capital!

He thought mainly about Mauritius and about all those he loved so much.

The British army had no precise information about the issue of this failed mission. Were they dead or alive, prisoners, or did they manage to escape? After some days without any news, the General Staff decided to alert their families and the news reached Mauritius like a bomb: *"Lieutenant Hyacinthe Wiehe is reported missing."*

The adults assembled at the tea hour, as usual, but with a downcast expression and without hiding their tears. With an immense sadness and a tremendous pain, they imagined the worst: *"Uncle Hyacinthe is reported missing? If the army says so it means it is serious. And if it is serious, it is because he is perhaps dead. How can we check that? What hope is there?"*

The brothers, too devastated, dared not announce anything to their mother. They then asked their sister Antoinette to transmit the news to her. The mother, with the strong faith that characterized her, just replied, while hiding her emotion: *"May God's Will be done!"*

As to Eda, so devastating was her pain that she thought she was going to die. She broke down on the steps of the Grand Baie Sailing Club, crying endlessly at the thought of her beloved.

For years she had dreaded such news! She would have liked so much to be at his side to take him in her arms, to care after him, to appease him. She imagined him dead, but held on with all her strength to the slightest hope left as long as she had not seen him dead and buried.

She wanted to see no one and no word could comfort her. All words twisted the knife in her wound. Drowned in her grief, she felt so lonely, so utterly abandoned. *"Life will have no meaning if Hyacinthe is dead, and if he dies, I prefer to die with him rather than live without him!"*

This state of mental torture prevailed amongst his closest ones who had to grow through long coming weeks without any news. They were torn between an obsessive fear of any eventual news of his death, which could have happened any time, and the hope of seeing him alive again.

Hyacinthe underwent an operation on 25 July, after three weeks of atrocious pains. He had often wondered if he would survive to his wounds. But he was blessed with an unsuspected strength to bear the trial. The operation was long and delicate, since the spinal marrow had not been spared. Two bullets of nine millimetres were extracted from his open wound

Around the same time, at the prison of the Place des Etats-Unis, captain Garstin was regaining hope. During one of the interrogations, the Germans had assured him that his companions and himself would be transferred to England by way of Switzerland, in exchange for German prisoners. This seemed to be worth believing and he managed to get an opportunity to pass this on to his friends. Rumour allowed the eventuality of a happy ending to their captivity, nevertheless not all of them welcomed it with the same enthusiasm, as it was not easy for them to give credit to their torturers' words.

On 8 August, several German officers visited them one by one, and, after a rapid inspection, they were able to wash themselves with hot water and soap. It was the first time since five weeks that they were allowed to feel good and clean!

The guards repeated what they had announced already: the prisoners would be led to Switzerland in order to serve as barter money for the freedom of German soldiers. They received civilian clothes, with the official pretext to appear less obtrusive. In spite of the bewilderment of a few of them, all hoped to see the end of their Calvary and some were even convinced of that!

During the night, towards one in the morning, handcuffed, and escorted by German officers, they were taken to a waiting truck in front of the main door of the building.

After only a few minutes along the sleepy roads of Paris, they reached the hospital of la Pitié-Salpêtrière. The only one of their group who could still be there would be Hyacinthe. Among the four who had been hospitalized on 5 July, that is a little more than three months before, one was dead, and two others had been led to prison, with them, after receiving medical care.

If Hyacinthe had suffered lighter wounds, he would have been in the truck, and this halt at the hospital would have had no sense. According to his fellow parachutists, it seemed obvious that the only plausible reason for this stop was to assemble all the surviving members of their group of twelve.

While the truck parked in the yard of the hospital, some slamming of doors sounded in the middle of the night. After a while, an unknown voice was heard. Someone was speaking to the driver and without knowing why, the truck started again, without Hyacinthe or anyone else.

After some time the truck stopped on the roadside. The last panels indicated the town of Beauvais. Anguish griped the group who were questioning the reason for this transit in open countryside, on the edge of a wood.

They were ordered to get out, and one by one, still handcuffed and escorted, they obeyed without resistance. The captain Garstin, who suffered from the sequel of his wounds, got out last, helped by one of his comrades.

In single file, they borrowed a path up in the woods while getting deeper towards the centre of the trees and bushes.

Daylight was appearing, whilst a strange impression of fear mixed with morning sweetness floated in the air.

After a walk of several minutes a voice cried out: *"My God! They are going to shoot us!"* Captain Garstin had not been able to hold back his fright upon arriving into the clearing, where his friends were already aligned like cattle to be slain.

He put himself in the ranks and faced, six or seven metres away the German soldiers accompanied by some civilians, one of whom read the judgment.

One soldier coldly translated: "You are found guilty of collaboration with the French terrorists, for the sabotage of the Reich's interests. You will therefore be treated as terrorists, and condemned to be shot."

Vaculick, the most intrepid of the group, could not bear the idea of being shot down in the middle of the forest, like an animal, after having borne all those terrible trials: the capture, the torture, the privations and the intimidations. He had already made several attempts to escape and this idea of escaping death was anchored in him, with a force and courage out of the ordinary. As soon as he understood the verdict, he tried all for all, to disappear in the forest by darting straight ahead.

Surprised by his reaction, the soldiers had not been able to shoot immediately, and when they tried to reach him, Vaculick threw himself to the ground and narrowly escaped the bullets that were whistling in his direction.

By crawling, he managed to sneak out and take flight through the thick bushes.

The others who had been aligned took advantage of this distraction to try to escape too. Less lucky, they fell one after the other under the bullets. Except one, Ginger, who stumbled against a root and fell during his run; but the Germans thought he was dead, shot by one of their bullets.

Within moments all the Nazis took the same direction as Vaculick to try to catch up with him. But after a long run through the woods and the fields, he succeeded in escaping from them.

These two survivors were able to give a detailed account, one in a book (Serge Vaculick, Beret Rouge), the other in a long letter sent to Hyacinthe, all that they had experienced since their landing in France till the day of their death sentence.

Hyacinthe had escaped death at least twice since his landing. Firstly at the time when he was hurt by the enemy shots, and then at that mysterious motherent when the truck had come to look for him with the condemned, to finally leave him behind.

He could not have learnt about the sad fate of his friends. Nor could he be aware of the disappearance of St-Exupery, the hero who had inspired him and of whom there were no more news since 31st July. Hyacinthe could no longer follow the stressful and tragic news of war, except a little bit through staff-members of the hospital.

The Wehrmacht in France was just being reorganized after the assassination attempt against the Fuhrer.

Among the new officers, many discovered France and its capital for the first time. In fact, they did not need to linger there as the retreat was already starting. First to leave were the administrative services, then the German civilians, on 9 and 10 August. The Résistance, consisting of Gaullists or Communists, had already started to prepare an uprising of the Parisian population. Shortages were expanding, black market exploding, food stocks becoming critical. Gasoline also was in cruel scarcity.

On 15 August, tension rose by several notches and everything accelerated. The municipal police went on strike. That same day, in some mysterious way, Hyacinthe was transferred from La Pitié-Salpêtrière to Rothschild Hospital. Why? The elements of an answer are presently still unclear and sometimes contradictory. Was it an error, or a friendly help?

It has never been solved in the end, but this was a motherent, which one could qualify today as of eternity. History was as if suspended by a mysterious intervention of Providence. One of the nurses, Madame Rosier, who had cared for Hyacinthe wrote him this letter dated 16 August:

My Lieutenant,

What a surprise, Wednesday 15 August at 15:00, while taking up my service of the 11th team at ground level, P.5. My colleagues wish me my feast day (Sainte Marie). Very touched by the kindness of my patients who offered me a superb bunch of flowers, and while I am thanking them for their gesture, my supervisor comes whispering to my ear that she has something for me that will please me much more.

I leave the room to follow her in her office, she hands me a letter: Yes, it was this letter written by you to the manager; I was so moved that I wept, excuse me for this weakness. For I esteemed you like a son, I regret only one thing, not having had the satisfaction of what I wanted for you. When I returned to La Pitié, you were gone in the morning. Finally, I am happy to know that your health is getting better and that you are among your own, ...

Much patience and courage in life: I wish you a good recovery; trust, God is good. Allow me to tell you that I shall never forget you in my prayers.

A nurse
M.L.Rosiers
If possible send me your news. Thank you.

Hyacinthe had therefore taken time to write a little thank you note to the management of the hospital. The nurse's answer attests how much it had been appreciated. Later, he traced Georges Leroux, a French Resistant wounded by the Germans, who shared his room at La Pitié-Salpêtrière. Through these little details the delicacy of Hyacinthe's character is unveiled. Although grievously wounded, he did not isolate himself, but considered every person he met as a providential relationship whom he had to take care of.

Why was he transferred? Who assured that transfer? In her letter, the nurse said that he was not there anymore on 15 August. However, according to the archives of the Parisian hospitals, he was admitted to Rothschild Hospital on 16 August.

On this feast of the Assumption of the Virgin Mary, he certainly benefited from a supernatural intervention of the Good Mother, whom he had prayed so much.

His arrival at the new hospital marked the beginning of a regained freedom. Hyacinthe was welcomed as a hero, as everybody was already convinced of the German capitulation. He was looked after more than he had ever been since his landing in France.

During this time, in the streets of Paris, where he had just travelled, tension was at its highest. The Allied Troops were approaching and the insurrection was being actively prepared.

A few days later, on 19 August, General Leclerc entered Paris and for the enemies it was the beginning of the end. One week was enough to liberate Paris.

On 26 August, General De Gaulle marched on the *Champs Elysées*, and then entered the *Notre-Dame-de-Paris* cathedral for a *Te-Deum*. For his part, Hyacinthe was praying and thanking God too. He was transferred again to *La Pitié-Salpêtrière* on 9 September.

At the same time in Mauritius, the crowds were converging towards Sainte-Croix, the burial place of Father Jacques Désiré Laval, Apostle of Mauritius.

Among the pilgrims was Antoinette Wiehe, accompanied by several members of her family. She had received some uncertain news about her son, a rumour that had reached the distant islands claiming that Hyacinthe was still alive. After two months of anguish and uncertainty, the whole family was hooked to this rumour. During this period the nights were sometimes very long and sleepless, when thoughts turned round and round in the heads and prevented sleep.

Hyacinthe, still prisoner of four walls and of his terrible pain, and despite the new freedom, was in a critical situation. He would have preferred to be one of those who were fighting, fighting for liberation. But he had to content himself to remain powerless and weak, without any weapon but his daily prayer, his perpetual prayer. He endured another combat in order to remain alive and see his own again: his island, his mother, and his beloved. But it was first in England that he was transferred on 27 September.

Marc Lagesse was the first in the family to give news of Hyacinthe. He did not hide his worries concerning his health, but he rejoiced for having found him while everybody thought he was dead:

After my arrival at London last week, I learnt first of all from R. who had lunched in Paris with one of the doctors of Hyacinthe's battalion, that the latter was reported missing and thought to be wounded and taken prisoner by the Germans. The next morning, I receive a letter from the chaplain of the hospital of the R.A.F. telling me that lieutenant Wiehe was out of danger. In my joy, I sent a cable (...) and exchanged several telegrams with Hyacinthe while making arrangements to visit him.

In the meantime, Éva Souchon goes to see him and phones to say that his condition is most serious, that it is feared he might lose the use of one of his legs, and that even his life may not be entirely safe.

Immediately, accompanied by Henri Rey to talk to the doctors, I went to see him. He has lost a lot of weight and his face is quite pale; they were getting ready to give him another blood transfusion.

He told us his story in detail: in brief, he had barely landed five minutes when a German machine-gun started to shoot at him. He received three bullets, one in the shoulder blade, one at the bottom of his spine, and the third one at the thigh.

The Germans captured him some hours later and he was transported to the German military hospital. Three weeks after his admission, he was operated on, and this only after all their own wounded had been taken care of.

Because of his name, he was taken for a Jew and was transferred to the Rothschild hospital, also in Paris. People were extremely kind to him there (...) It is there that the Americans found him when they arrived in Paris (...).

His spirits are excellent. He is in a sort of euphoria caused, without doubt, by the morphine. He is not conscious of his condition and we have prepared at length a program of celebrations when he will leave the hospital. He is obviously very weak and cannot read or write. He eats anything he wants and that pleases him. He has remained the dear gentleman that we have learnt to love so much. With his trembling hands, he has searched through his papers for the address of a guy who had lent him some money in Paris so that I do the necessary (...) He has preserved his faculties entirely; his memory is perfect. We have chatted and laughed like in old times.

Here is now the medical analysis. The wounds at the shoulder blade and thigh are not serious. Only the spine one is cause for worry. Unfortunately, the surgical operation and the relevant X-rays were performed by the Germans, and nothing is known here.

If the bullet has only displaced one of the bones of the spine without damaging the spinal marrow itself, he will get over it after some time. But if the bullet has touched the marrow, there is very little hope. As far as the doctors know here, they fear that unfortunately it may be the second alternative.

Hyacinthe however complains of pains in his legs, which is, apparently, a very good sign. He is entirely plastered, except for the top part of the body. He will be moved again to go to a hospital specialized in this case of spinal marrow, the hospital being quite close to London, we shall be able to see him more often.

Following this letter from Marc, the news spread in a short time. The cousins and friends who were in England came to visit him and check out his condition for themselves.

In Mauritius, all were relieved. Antoinette, his mother, turned instinctively towards Heaven and did not stop repeating: *"Thank You! Thank You! Thank You!"*

She did not hide her emotion.

The brothers got together to celebrate the news, even though they still worried about his condition.

Eda jumped for joy and hurried to Labourdonnais to rejoice with the family! She felt her body shake with emotion.

"He is alive! He is alive!" She could not repress that immense joy which burst from within.

After having taken time to kiss the whole family and share all the good news, she could not help withdrawing, to take a walk towards the old orchard. There, in the midst of the birds' concert, she stopped in front of a mango-tree. That tree of promise was the place where she wanted to celebrate alone this great news! *"He is alive! He will come back!"*

It was all that was needed for her to express her happiness. In this burst of emotion, she could not help huddle against the tree and hug it with her arms. Then, she made a few steps back to look at this mango-tree, which had never looked so pretty!

"What a beautiful day! What a relief!"

A few days later, Eda took the road of *'Sans Souci'* and wanted to walk alone on the paths where they had ventured together, in the filaos woods, and up to the beach of *Anse-La-Raie*. Everything was alive once more; everything was merry again, even if the wait would be long before seeing her beloved!

The first mail from Hyacinthe to his mother, written with a trembling hand, was on 22 October 1944:

I unite you to the family, my very dear Mother, to tell you my most affectionate wishes. I am still feeling better. I shall try to write to you soon. I kiss you very affectionately. H.

Another letter was written to Eda, simply to tell her his love. His case remained worrying and he preferred not to discuss it. Indeed, he suffered persistent fevers and a urinary infection. A *bacillum pyocyanic* was detected, very difficult to treat and leading to death in half of the cases. He also had many bedsores and on arrival in England, medical reports signalled a form of depression.

As soon as he could, he wrote his first letter, in longer terms, addressed to his mother:

3 December 1944

My very dear Mother,

I will try to scribble a few lines, now that it seems to me possible to start writing again. I would like to start by thanking you, as well as the family, for the many cables and letters which in the present circumstances give me double pleasure; for your prayers too which, I am certain, have helped me so much to go through times that were sometimes quite rough. I felt it from the motherent when I was wounded.

How would I have been able to overcome the first shock, confront the treatments that were not always adequate that I received afterwards, avoid going with some of my companions to Germany, if I was not protected?

As you must have learnt, I fell into a trap prepared by the Gestapo, a few minutes after landing in France. I shall not tell you about the subsequent events, which finally brought me back to England: maybe others have already told you about them, and then, what's the use of reviving those moments?

How describe my joy on seeing Eva again, who rushed to the Wroughton Hospital as soon as she learnt that I was there.

And now that I am at Leatherhead, she comes to spend one hour every day with me, bringing me every time a little treat; as aunt Edith says, she is the real *'angel of the family'*.

(...) You must already know that I have made great progress since my arrival here, progress that the doctors even qualify as surprising! There still remain however quite many long months to endure with patience - with a little courage I shall succeed in going through them. Already, the pains, which since five months have never left me, seem to diminish now. I have to say that I am well taken care of by the doctors and the nurses, who, I am conscious now, have brought me back from quite far, have saved my life, I should say.

In a letter of 25 October 1944, a friend of the family gave the news confirming those that he had sent by cable.

He wrote to Hyacinthe's brother:

My dear Georges, I confirm to you my telegrams concerning Hyacinthe. I am happy that he has been able to be transferred to Leatherhead for Eva and Marie can take care of him. Eva visits him daily (...) The poor friend has been grievously wounded and unfortunately the Leatherhead specialist confirms the fact that Hyacinthe will remain crippled even if he survives (...) My heart goes to you my dear friends, in your anguishes concerning Hyacinthe - my thought goes in particular to your dear mother who must suffer so much for not being close to her son during these painful days.

It is a real blessing that Eva arrived here on time, for she is so good and devoted, it is a great comfort for Hyacinthe.

The same day, on 25 October 1944, Eva wrote a letter to her aunt Antoinette:

I am sure, my dear aunt, that it is your prayers and those of all yours that have obtained such considerably great graces for

Hyacinthe. His patience is admirable, and during the cramps that take him at the knees he controls himself admirably. He told me recently: "When you write to mother, tell her about my life here."

He is in a large room, which is, I can say, almost familial: an atmosphere of friendship prevails here. There are big heating devices in the middle of the room. Flowers brighten it. Hyacinthe's bed is almost in the middle of the room, to the right side.

His dressings are changed for the first time at 5:30 am, and all in all four times daily. I always wait till the 2:30 pm one has been done before going to the hospital. He does not appreciate much this early morning wake-up, but it is certain that he is aware of all the good that these constant cares provide him. (...) Hyacinthe has certainly had the tremendous luck of having been forgotten by the Germans, who, he told me, made an error by sending him to the Rothschild Hospital!!! They could have fetched him back there = then what happened? No one knows, but the Gestapo did not come back to get him!! At Rothschild the FFI welcomed him with honour. Two of them came to thank him for what he had done, and, to his great uneasiness, they kissed him!

He was treated with champagne and a lady, very kind towards him, has even offered one of her crystal glasses, as Hyacinthe had mentioned the lack of charm of drinking champagne from a bowl! (...)

Your dear son! My darling aunt, how I would rather love you to have the happiness of being near him every day! I can assure you that Marie and I have a great affection for him, and are happy that he is near us.

Today I receive your nice letter of the 19th August and you magnificent gift for Marie, Maurice and me. I do not find enough words to thank you my dear aunt. How good, too good, you are. Marie and I are infinitely touched. Thank you again with all our heart.

I kiss you with all my tenderness. Eva

Take good care of your health my dear aunt. We are in union of prayers, always.

Marie and Eva Souchon were two sisters, daughters of Louis Souchon and Georgina Rouillard, the latter a sister of Antoinette Wiehe, Hyacinthe's mother. Marie was born in 1894, and Eva in 1903. They were respectively 50 and 39 years old, when their young first-degree cousin arrived in England. Their devotion to him was remarkable, as the preceding mails can attest.

Marie had married Noel Couve de Murville. Both born in Mauritius, they had migrated first to France, then to England.

As to Eva, she remained single. She thus had more time than her sister to visit Uncle Hyacinthe every day. She remained all her life devoted to the service of others around her.

On 21 May 1946, Marie was going to die prematurely, and it was Eva who raised her nephews. Among them, Maurice, born on 27 June 1929. He was 17 years old at the death of his mother and oriented himself towards priesthood. Ordained on 29 June 1957, he became Archbishop of Birmingham on 22 January 1982 till his retirement in 1999.

Marc Lagesse also died tragically. His sister Maud had married Marc, Hyacinthe's brother with whom he had always been close. Marc had enrolled in the British army too. He had realized his dream of becoming an aviator. Alas, his fate was dramatic. On 10 January 1945, at the heart of a mission, his plane crashed accidentally, and there was no survivor.

His sister, who was affectionately called *Mimi*, remembered perfectly the announcement of his death. Some members of the family - including her - were sitting around a game table, with their mother, when someone entered with a dramatic look on his face.

Marc's mother got up then, asking all those present to kneel down: "*Let's ask the Virgin Mary to give us the strength to receive this news.*"

All therefore prayed an Ave Maria. Then, rising, she asked: "*Is it concerning Marc?*"

"*Yes*", answered the visitor.

"Is he dead?"

"Yes", he replied...

Mimi had never forgotten this incident announcing the tragic death of her brother aged 27.

They were at *Grand Baie*, next to *Mont Choisy*, the spot where a great crowd had watched with fascination the first airplane landing in Mauritius, some years back.

Marc could not therefore celebrate the Victory with Hyacinthe as they had imagined when they had been reunited at the hospital. Tragic destiny! Dramatic issue of a war that had come all the way to Mauritius to snatch a few youths from their families and from their native land!

Vocation

February 1945.

The Yalta Conference had started. The world leaders were preparing the post-war while Hyacinthe, on his side, was preparing to go back to Mauritius and to his own. He was already getting a little better and communicated more regularly with his close ones. In a letter to his brother Ernest, he narrated how presently he managed to sit down after a period of convalescence that had lasted six months.

In a cable dated February 1945, he wanted to reassure his mother concerning his health:

Eva must have told you that a new crisis overtook me recently. It's getting better, I must say, and now I can again go outside and take some fresh air on my chair, (...) Don't worry about the care I am receiving. I'm very well treated, and I can even say that one of the doctors in charge of me is probably the most famous specialist in England in his field.

Everybody was waiting for Hyacinthe's return to the country, after all those years of painful separation. They were eager to turn the page, to start a new chapter, even though they were well aware that things could not anymore get back to what they were before.

In September 1945, as soon as Hyacinthe's imminent departure was being organised, Arthur de Chazal, Hyacinthe's brother-in-law, shared his objections and his worry. As he practised medicine in Mauritius he knew well the limitations of the hospital institutions of the island: he was of the opinion that the quality of healthcare was not good enough to treat a patient seriously injured at war.

Hyacinthe too was conscious of that, and had anticipated this difficulty, for fear that it be an obstacle that would keep him nailed to England for the rest of his life.

According to the specialists in charge of his care, the presence of a good nurse at his side seemed of the first importance. He absolutely needed someone who was well trained, and available, so as to provide him with all necessary daily care. As a coincidence, he had made the acquaintance of Kathleen Ruscoe, who worked at the hospital of Leatherhead. For a long time he had noticed her dedication, and, as was his custom, Hyacinthe had shown empathy towards her, towards her life marked by a great tragedy: all her family had perished during the London air raids some years back. She was left alone in the world, and thereupon her whole life was dedicated only to war-wounded patients.

This total dedication brought a sense to her life, helped her not to break down in ultimate misery.

In the course of one of their conversations, little and brief exchanges, but so precious for the solitary patients, Hyacinthe had sensed her distress. He could share the existential questions that troubled her inwardly: how live when all the loved ones are dead? Where settle down in order not to think of this nightmare? What should one do in order to remain standing and move forward?

He had made a serious proposal to her, without mentioning it too early to his close ones. Hyacinthe had explained to Kathleen his situation, asking her to accompany him to Mauritius and stay at his side so that he could receive care. Kathleen had never imagined going to the end of the world in the colonies. But with some hindsight and time to think it over, she agreed, having no more reason to live in England. It was agreed that she would stay long enough to train someone else who would then replace her, and that after such a period, she would be free to choose: either to go back to Europe or stay in Mauritius.

It was only fifteen days before Hyacinthe's departure that the family was informed of the presence of 'Sister' who would accompany him. 'Sister' was the surname that Kathleen would keep henceforth, quite a usual name for a nurse.

After a long journey by ship, and many stops - the last one in South Africa, Hyacinthe arrived in Mauritius in February 1946.

When approaching the Mauritian coasts, great was his emotion as he saw the land at the horizon. It was hot and humid; the sea glittered. The band of land at the horizon increased in size, and he recognized certain localities of the island. He perceived the North Plain with all the emerging memories coming back. He saw the high plateaux and felt the tears of joy. Never before the sight of a land had inspired such an emotion in him! This island that was approaching was his little corner of paradise on earth, not only for its natural beauty, but above all for the people living there and whom he loved above everything else in the world.

The ship was now at the harbour's entrance and a tug accompanied it. While entering the port, he remembered those explorers who, for centuries, had come to this extinct volcano in the middle of the Indian Ocean. He remembered the stories that had enchanted his childhood, but imagined also the drama of those ships that had been wrecked on the reefs, at some hundred metres off the coasts, such as the Saint Géran which was bringing Virginie back to Paul.

Everybody was on the quay to welcome him: his brothers, his sister and his brother-in-law, several of his nephews and nieces, his friends, his mother, and his beloved Eda who was quivering with a strange sensation: a deep joy mixed with a secret apprehension.

That day had been waited for since more than five years: for everyone it had looked like an eternity. An important number of Mauritians had gathered to welcome back their close ones to the country. Everyone was waiving a hat or a handkerchief to greet this ship that was arriving, like a god of the seas bringing to safe harbour those dear beings who had disappeared at the horizon a few years before.

The authorities had organised a special shuttle, more comfortable, to transport Hyacinthe on his stretcher. But the latter refused this preferential treatment. Gone with everyone, he wanted to come back with all those who were coming back to the country, without any favour. He had been adamant about that, as he had feared also to alarm his close relatives and thus dramatize his condition.

On the quays, the people were scrutinizing the ship for the one they were waiting for. As the faces became clearer, the crowd's exclamations grew louder. Arthur only had been able to have access to the landing point to take part in the medical assistance. And the others had still to be patient, scrutinizing at some ten metres away the movements of all those who were returning to their land and to their families.

Hyacinthe was identified and settled in an ambulance. He was not laid entirely flat on the stretcher: the back was slightly brought up, so that his chest and his head could be seen. Everyone called each other with excitement, but several felt a shudder of anguish at the sheer sight of reality: Hyacinthe was coming back paralyzed!

The family and the close ones were able to approach for a brief moment of greetings. The friends, very respectful, stayed a little at the back to allow the family to come forward. The brothers and sisters were all present, forming a group to support each other, holding their mother with affection. But his mother, concerned about Eda, signalled her with her eyes to approach too.

Nothing else in the world counted more than these reunions. Tears were shed, hugs exchanged with a rare intensity! Nothing and no one in Mauritius was more precious than the one who was coming back from so far!

The staff had to be careful that Hyacinthe would not be overtired. Sister encountered the ones and the others; she was a little shy at finding herself all of a sudden at the heart of a family intimacy.

Eda refrained herself in front of all those present: she would have liked so much to express her joy and her love, but also her sorrow to see him in such a condition! His mother thanked God in the depth of her heart, and all were fretful as emotion was so strong. Hyacinthe, as to him, was feeling so light that he had the impression of flying. His happiness was just indescribable!

That priceless moment had to be shortened for the medical staff to do their work. Which suited everybody, for to some extent uneasiness prevailed too; no appropriate words could be found to express what was felt deep down in the hearts. One of his brothers threw a joke to de-dramatize the situation, so that laughter would express what could not be said otherwise.

The procession started on its way. The ambulance took the direction of the Vacoas hospital and cars followed. The two rear doors were left open, so that Hyacinthe would enjoy the landscape passing by, but especially the faces of those who had followed him up till then by way of letters and telegrams, and who were now so close, physically present.

His face was enlightened with an intense happiness. He could not help smiling from ear to ear and gesturing with his hand during the entire trip to the hospital. Some and others reciprocated, the children in the cars were ecstatic such a scenario!

Arthur had had the time to look rapidly through the medical file while waiting for the landing formalities.

He dared not say anything, but from what he had read in the reports, Hyacinthe was in a critical state and, according to him, could not hence live very long. He imagined already his brother in law's death, and thought that it would be soon.

Mauritius was no longer the same since the end of the war. The scars were there, hidden in the families and in the hearts of those who had suffered from the deaths or wounds of their close ones, but also from the consequences of malnutrition or illness.

Surely, those sufferings could not be compared to those of countries and peoples devastated by the unfurling of violence, and ruined in all points of view. But in Mauritius, as elsewhere, one had to start again, bounce back, rebuild an economy and a social life. One had to turn the page of war and try a new impetus.

An aerodrome, Plaisance, had been built hastily by the English, at the time when Japan entered the war and when the battlefields extended to the distant seas, well beyond Europe. Ships had resumed their rhythm in Port-Louis's harbour, but little by little aviation was going to develop and change Mauritian life progressively.

Hyacinthe's close relatives had to show a lot of patience. The military procedures required that he should first be hospitalized for medical examinations.

Hyacinthe took advantage of this to ask for his formal demobilization. It became effective a few months later.

After this time of observation at the Vacoas hospital, he was able to move into his new apartments, which had been set up in the house at Floréal.

Among those who were looking for an authorization to meet him, Eda just could not wait. As soon as he was settled in the ground floor at his mother's place, she rushed to pay him a visit, in the course of the afternoon, after the cares of the mid-day.

Hyacinthe welcomed her, seated in his wheel chair and with a blanket placed over his knees, covering his thighs from hips to feet. He was clean-shaven, hair neatly styled, smiling, wearing his most beautiful shirt that hid his lean arms.

The room smelled cleanliness; it had been tidied. Sister went outside after welcoming Eda, prescribing that the visit should not be not too long, so as not to tire him. But the beloved did not want to listen to these regulations that she judged a little too exaggerated, and their conversation started simply, from the arrival of the ship a few days before, going over those much anticipated reunions. The room where they were was illuminated by the happiness that was within them.

They looked at each other with intensity, every single detail of their face being mutually admired.

Their glances were replete with immense affection. Each one felt a thirst that could be quenched by holding to each other, straight in the eyes.

Eda did not resist the desire to hold his hand and they began talking about their feelings, about what they had gone through far from each other.

Time passed and they were satiated by this moment of intimacy when suddenly Hyacinthe let go brutally of Eda's hand. He tensed more and more, closing his eyes with all his strength, face pain-contorted, tense, changing colour. His suffering was palpable! Eda was seized with panic and rushed in the adjacent room to look for Sister who arrived immediately. She told her that this was going to pass, that it was normal, that she would have to be familiar with those pain crisis.

With dexterity, Sister took Hyacinthe's arm with one hand, while verifying, with her other hand, the presence of medication and water. This crisis lasted long minutes. Eda was inwardly distraught, but Sister's calmness helped her to regain control on herself.

When this torture ended, she remained at a little distance and dared not talk anymore. Hyacinthe calmed down, straightened up and looked at her lovingly. She plunged her eyes into his: with them, she expressed her interrogation concerning that mysterious journey to the heart of suffering. Hyacinthe smiled and said some nice words to reassure her. But Sister made Eda understand that it was better if her visit ended.

Embarrassed, perplexed, she left the room in silence, after having said good-by to her fiancé. The latter was so sad to see her leave. He was broken, as he would have liked to keep her but he felt that he needed to rest. While Sister prepared his bed, he could not control himself and wept loudly.

Never had Sister seen him cry like that.

She felt his sorrow, but he, on his part, did not want to talk to anyone. It had been so nice to see Eda again, he would have so much liked to be able to go out and walk alongside her everywhere she wished to go.

Other visits were going to follow one after another in a natural way. Everybody wanted to see Hyacinthe again, but all were extremely surprised by the violence of his pain crisis, which broke out very frequently, without warning.

His brothers could not help talking about their childhood, to reawaken common memories, to laugh out loud! But they always had to come back to the grim reality, and leave their brother who needed to rest.

His mother visited him several times a day, but she soon understood the drama that was taking place. Hyacinthe had come back to his own people, but he would have to die to himself, as he had to when he had left for the war, and now with even more certainty. Her son had come back to his country, to his family, to his fiancée, to his friends….But somehow, as he seemed to retrieve his lost happiness, he would have to renounce quite a lot of things and people, so dear to him, and stay in his mutilated body as in a prison!

His friends came regularly at the beginning, but many dared not disturb him after witnessing those staggering pain manifestations that caused them embarrassment.

Sister saw to it that the visits were well regulated, and not exhausting for him. Seeing her exemplary dedication to Hyacinthe, she was respected by all.

Day and night, she stayed in proximity, watching over the details of his health: his food, his medication, his times of rest, and especially his dressings done many times a day, which required much precision and professionalism.

Arthur passed by regularly to examine him. He was particularly fond of his visits to Hyacinthe, for there emanated from that room a peace and a serenity, which he had rarely seen elsewhere. Yet, in an objective way, the situation was dramatic. But peace prevailed more and more, and the conversations were always deep, full of friendship and truth.

Eda did everything she could to come as often as possible, despite the difficulty for her to bear Hyacinthe's health condition and to see him suffer. She thought that Sister was upset about seeing her come so often but she could not help it. Her life without Hyacinthe had no sense, and even if he was a prisoner of that paralysis which weighed down on his body and on all his life, she felt like a disabled person if she could not see him often enough.

Circumstances were becoming more and more pathetic. They loved each other so much that they needed to see each other again and again. But each of their encounters ended in tears. Each time they both felt torn apart. She left, crying loud, to shut herself in her room. And as to him, he did not want any visit anymore and was getting depressed.

They imagined that things would get better, that he would perhaps walk again some day and live a normal life again. They told themselves that science would surely make some progress and that he would be cured, or a miracle was still possible.

They could not help it. They hang on desperately to that desire of resuming their life where they had left it, before the war separated them, of marrying and starting a family. That so soft, so comforting dream, had allowed them to bear the most anguishing conditions during those years of war! This aspiration had been nourished, entertained, cultivated in many ways in their imagination and in their correspondence. But this dream seemed to vanish at the end of each visit, like a mirage which disappeared, leaving place to the so cruel reality of a life of physical sufferings, and the impossibility to build a long term relationship.

Sister took to heart her nursing mission, which was completed by her functions as a night-watchwoman, governess, and secretary to regulate the visits.

However her daily life was quite austere, monotonous and solitary. She spent a lot of time alone in her room, plunged into her readings or in her thoughts. Her only true friend was Mrs Vaughan, who invited her regularly, thereby giving her the opportunity to meet a compatriot again, to get out of her daily routine during a few hours.

Mrs Vaughan's husband, Reginald, had a passion for Mauritius endemic plants, of which he made an inventory. He even made some exciting discoveries and certain plants bear his name.

Mr Reginald Vaughan was a great friend and close collaborator of Octave Wiehe, Hyacinthe's brother, founder of the 'Mauritius Sugarcane Industry Research Institute' (MSIRI), and first vice-chancellor of the University of Mauritius.

Sister had some difficulty to adapt to this new social context, and she appreciated the change of air when with the season change, Antoinette and her crippled son left Floréal for their long annual stay at Labourdonnais.

In order to accommodate Hyacinthe and his nurse there, a special pavilion was built and set up next to the chateau, just to the right of the entrance by the alley of intendance trees. Until recently, one could still see the foundations of this modest but very cute cottage, built in wood, thatch and *ravenale*, that fibre that is extracted from the traveller's palm. It was situated in the direction of the orchard, not far from Antoinette's window, for she wanted to stay in the proximity of her suffering son.

On arrival at Labourdonnais, Hyacinthe sensed he was coming back to life. He really felt at home in this family domain, where he had grown up and where he could commune with nature at heart full.

He went out more easily to enjoy the large garden. The birds came to him and he fed them. He liked so much these moments with them! Since his return to Mauritius, he was even more fascinated by their number and ever presence which cheered the atmosphere. He observed them in full flight and could not help trying to imagine the view they had from the sky, remembering his own plane trips.

Contemplating their gracefulness and their movements, he was thinking back of those sensations felt in the atmosphere, when he was softly coming down under his parachute. But what he liked most was their song. He recognised the martins and the cardinals, the *bul-buls* and the *Cape's canaries...* And his favourite song was the turtledove's one:

"The sweetness of the little turtle's song makes me feel good," he used to say.

Those outdoors moments were much appreciated, but he had to spend most of his time inside his pavilion.

From his window, he paid attention to the particular atmosphere prevailing outside, listened to the slightest sound, which helped him to travel in his mind. He heard the workers who were busy preparing the sugarcane harvest.

His brothers passed by regularly and fed him with news of the domain: the state of the fields, of the factory engines, of the staff; he knew many of them.

Eda carried on visiting him, less often, but regularly.

They were both appeased and faced the situation more easily. They did everything they could to try not to keep their old dreams alive, to entertain a beautiful friendship by giving up the idea of starting a family.

Her visits were often interrupted by pain crisis that she bore henceforth with more courage, until the day that she cracked.

They had been able to go out for a short time and proceeded slowly towards the orchard.

Eda was pushing the wheelchair and Hyacinthe was continuing the conversation while admiring the nature. Titch, Hyacinthe's little fox terrier was following them.

At the sight of their mango-tree, that tree which symbolized the promises associated with their love, Eda could not contain her sadness and broke down. She loved Hyacinthe so much, and this promenade in the afternoon light evoked too many memories that she felt difficult to forget.

He had upheld his promise and he was back, but she would never be able to marry him, to be his wife and the mother of his children!

She could not control her emotion and they were both shattered. It was like a wound that had started to heal and which was reopening abruptly and bleeding. Their hearts were mortally wounded and that suffering which they felt drew them even closer, united them even more, but they could not speak anymore.

They had to come back to the pavilion and Sister noticed their uneasiness. Eda was embarrassed and took her leave. They had the impression of going back to their point of departure, to experience the same distress that had struck them in the weeks following Hyacinthe's return. They had tried to overcome the trial but it came back again in a more powerful way, and they did not know how to face it again.

Sister felt this torment that was defeating him again, and depressing him, so she understood on that day that their relationship had to stop definitively.

During those stays at Labourdonnais, many cousins met in the gardens. Two of his brothers lived there permanently with their respective families: Georges, who was the administrator, and Adrien, a renowned engineer who worked both on the family property and other domains of the island. Another of his brothers, Ernest, lived at a few kilometres on the property of Ferret.

The nephews and nieces were numerous, exclusive of those who came regularly from Curepipe, with Marc, or from Reduit, with Octave, or still the bunch of cousins of the third generation. There were always gangs of children and teenagers who were having the time of their lives in the gardens. They had regularly to be called to order by the adults, when their shouts became excessive:

"Enough kids! Hyacinthe is resting!"

Hyacinthe was at his rest certainly, but he did not really complain about the shouts, even when they were sometimes a little too loud. On the contrary, it did him good to hear them as they evoked memories of his own childhood when he could run about, carefree, in those magical corners around the chateau!

Ah! How sweet were those childhood races, when trotting among the flowers, or admiring the gloxinias on the balustrades, or climbing up the trees to pick some fruits, or playing among the branches, looking for the best corners to build a little hut or even to hide!

His nephews needed an authorisation from the adults to visit him.

The official visit occurred generally on Sunday after the 8:30 mass at Pamplemousses. It was a festive opportunity for the youngest ones, who then were offered arrow-root biscuits, a specialty of the domain, that their grandmother treasured in a metal box.

When she received her grandchildren and their parents, she used to verify if her paralyzed son was fit enough for a visit or not.

She was treated with respect and affection and assembled her own regularly for family councils. Her children loved her very much and they always assembled with great willingness for family meals, or teas on the veranda.

Whenever he could, Hyacinthe participated a little in those moments full of affection, shared passions, animated discussions, and jokes which ended with loud and endless laughter. And even if he could not always be present, the warmth of those family gatherings was a great support to him.

In the conversations, they spoke about everything, except the war. For him it was a nightmare, which he had to forget, a trauma which, though wearing off with time, could not necessarily be wiped out from his memory.

He sometimes thought about his comrades in the British army, especially those with whom he was keeping an epistolary relationship

Gradually Hyacinthe had to face the obvious - his relation with Eda had no future.

They had hoped to get married, but it was not possible. They had tried to remain friends, but this was too difficult. He did not know how to face this additional trial: he was in a deadlock. Thanks to his mother's support, he managed to put words on what he felt. In a very tactful way, she managed to find the appropriate words to share in his suffering and to respect his choice of breaking up with Eda.

That separation was tremendously hard for both of them. Their last meeting was particularly pathetic. Eda had wrapped her engagement ring that she had worn for more than six years! That ring was the most valuable item she had, not for its gold or its precious stone, but rather for all the love that it symbolized:

that was her treasure, and the promise that it contained had entertained her hope. Giving back that ring was like amputating one of her members. A part of her was torn away.

Immediately after leaving it, she ran away without turning back. On the advice of her close relatives, she then decided to leave for France for a long recovery, in order to try to get her fiancé out of her mind.

Shortly after that, she, in turn, embarked on a ship that was going to Europe. She thought that she would not come back to Mauritius. Indeed, it seemed impossible for her to live in proximity of her ex-fiancé whom she still loved tremendously.

Hyacinthe suffered a serious blow too. Supported by his friends, he tried to resume some drawing to occupy his mind, in order not to sink into despair.

He received some commissions from his former colleagues and he was happy to be able to take his architectural instruments out, to use his expertise in the service of others. In fact, this was helping him to some extent, although his limited physical capacities did not allow him to invest much of himself in his work.

Thanks to his faith, he learnt how to deal with this renunciation, and to enter with his whole being into a new form of vocation, a very particular one.

Uncle Hyacinthe had never stopped nourishing his faith through his daily prayer and his frequent readings. He ordered books from France regularly, and had got himself a magnificent Bible that helped him to meditate the Word of God.

Moreover, he gained support from Father Keenan, who visited him regularly, thus giving him an opportunity to receive the sacraments of the Eucharist and of Confession. This priest was a friend of the family.

Irish by nationality, he had been ordained for the diocese of Port-Louis.

He knew Hyacinthe who had been his pupil at Pere Laval College between 1926 and 1930. When the school was closed down, he was appointed at Poudre d'Or and Rivière du

Rempart, and had the Sainte Claire chapel built at Goodlands. From there, he interacted with the Wiehe family. Particularly close to Georges, he visited Labourdonnais quite regularly.

In 1940, he was moved to Phoenix and when Hyacinthe came back to Mauritius, it was obviously Father Keenan who was invited to visit the war wounded who was back in the country.

What they had said to each other will be forever kept secret, but Fr. Keenan's support was a precious gift, when for instance he had to renounce his fiancée. This choice had been dictated as much by reason as by a call to enter into a new stage, another life dimension.

It is difficult to exactly situate in time this interior shift, but his membership in the Union Sainte Anne on one hand, and in Amicitia on the other hand, provide us with some indications.

The Union Sainte Anne originated from Sainte-Anne-de-Beaupré's sanctuary, in Quebec. On a card signed by Hyacinthe's hand and dated 17th October 1946, one can read the following prayer addressed to Saint Ann for his cure:

"Grant that I be delivered from my disabilities, and that I may be able to consecrate my re-established forces to the service of God and of my neighbour. How sweet it would be if I could proclaim that I owe to your intercession the return of a health which, by attesting your mercy towards me, would become, maybe, for many souls, a cause for conversion."

But this first part of the prayer was never granted. Was Heaven deaf to his calls? No, certainly not! The prayer went on with other invocations that, for their part, were granted:

"But I desire above all to abandon myself to the Will of God... Grant me this grace that I love God more and more, when my trials extend and get worse. Such a miracle is greater than would be the suddenness of my cure. It is easier for God to cure my suffering than to make me love it."

God's omnipotence was going to be manifested into his inmost self, not to transform his mortally wounded body, but to change his heart, and give it new capacities to believe, to hope, and to love. At the time when he found himself in such a great vulnerability, a new force was going to support him.

At the end of 1946, on the 8th December precisely, Hyacinthe joined another fellowship: *Amicitia, Union of the sick.*

This admission was authenticated by a card, signed by the 'great sister', Jeanne Archambault, the general director.

At the bottom of the signature, two biblical verses:

"*Love one another*", and *"I am full of joy in my sufferings and what is missing in the sufferings of Christ, I complete it in my own flesh for his body which is the Church"* (Saint Paul, Colossians 1,24)

The 'Great Sister of Amicitia' was known in France for her zeal to be at the service of the sick, even though she herself had a delicate health, which had degenerated to the point of confining her to a wheelchair.

The work started in 1920 by a Vosgienne, Miss Wiltz, who wished to establish a network among the sick to prevent them from feeling lonely, and give them the opportunity to help each other materially and spiritually.

The inspirational place was Lourdes, where an impressive number of invalids and sick got together to make a pilgrimage to the grotto of Massiabelle.

Several years later, approved by its bishop in 1922, Amicitia had become a network of about five hundred sick, accompanied by several chaplains, and sharing a small liaison bulletin. One of those chaplains knew Jeanne Archambault and the latter joined the work, first as a member, then rapidly as a director and 'great sister'.

At the end of the war, her family had lost everything but she found the inner resources to support every member and to dedicate herself more and more to helping the sick.

In this after-war period, when a great number of people were bearing in their flesh the marks of the conflict, the work developed considerably. The first grand pilgrimage of Amicitia to Lourdes occurred in 1947.

The spirituality transmitted by the Work was going to nourish Hyacinthe and enlighten his vocation. In one of the first brochures one could read:

"To suffer is the lot of all at Amicitia. But to offer oneself, and, from that to smile, is only possible by a union to the mission of Christ that continues in his Church: it is essentially a redemption mission. And because the Virgin has offered herself totally, because Our Lord has made her the Mediator of all graces for us, the spirituality of the sick of Amicitia is a Marian mysticism."

This spirituality does not consist of masochism, glorified suffering, or a form of satisfaction in suffering. It is a path to handle the evil, to go beyond it, to use it as a springboard in order to propel oneself with a greater love and fervour towards God and towards the service of one's neighbour. This all-Marian spirituality is the secret of the poor in spirit, a revelation received by the little ones, those who are truly humble.

In a village of the Drôme in France, a woman was a great living proof of this spirituality: Marthe Robin offered herself to God in the darkness of her bedroom, without eating any food. In 1927, she wrote:

"Suffering is the incomparable school of true love".

Marthe testified to this spirituality centred not on suffering, but on Jesus-Christ and his paradoxical teaching:

"Blessed are those who mourn, for they will be comforted"; "Blessed are they who are persecuted for the sake of justice for the Kingdom of Heaven is theirs".

Hyacinthe journeyed deep down his soul, to seek and find in himself that hidden door, that narrow door which opened onto new lights. It was his special secret to find a new dimension for his life, characterised by an ability to face with more confidence and more love those physical and moral sufferings afflicting him. By joining Amicitia, he supported the purpose of the Work, which was thus defined:

"Amicitia wishes to help the sick to bear their sufferings, to make them understand the value of their trial – a precious Cross - and teach them how to enrich it by making it, through their apostolate, contribute to their personal sanctification as well as to their brothers' - the sick.

For this, it wants to be - above all for the sick, the infirm, often so lonely, for the 'ones with poor health ', also so often isolated or abandoned - for all those souls, it wants to be 'a family' where they can feel being understood, helped and tenderly, fraternally loved in Christ-Jesus.

All sick persons are admitted regardless of age, ailments, or social condition. It is a family whose doors are heartily open to all. "

This enrolment helped a young Mauritian to join a new family. He could not meet the official members, most of them being in France, nor the potential members spread all around the world, but through this he joined a true chain of prayer and mutual support, entered a new vocation which was henceforth going to influence the rest of his life and give it a meaning. He often took part in the *grand'messe des malades* (High Mass of the Sick) at the Sanctuary of *Marie Reine de la Paix* (Mary Queen of Peace).

During some more auspicious years, Hyacinthe tried to move around in a black Morris Minor, especially adapted for a handicapped person.

In that car, the controls for accelerating and braking are manual. He was without doubt among the only ones in Mauritius to benefit from this technological advance. Thus, he tasted a little bit of freedom, visiting some family members or friends.

He parked it in front of the houses, and while he remained in his car, his hosts welcomed him, sat on their front-steps, and conversed with him for a moment, as if there was nothing strange about this.

This feeling of freedom was cut short by the deterioration of his health. The wound at the bottom of his back was hard to heal completely. He then suffered from uraemia, and one of his hips had to be removed: bedsores appeared now and then, as well as other small complications linked to his particular case.

Arthur, who continued to provide him care, often repeated: *"His life is a mystery!"*

Legacy

Months passed by and Hyacinthe was growing in a deeper intimacy with God, a better acceptance of his suffering, and a greater irradiation of his faith. He had understood that he had to renounce the idea of recovering his body's good health. But above all, that he had to engage in a new fight which would introduce him to new spiritual forces and into paths hitherto unsuspected.

That path had not been treaded without difficulties. It could be said that it had even been a true crossing of the desert! He had known the Egyptian desert and its mirages, the vast expanses of sand that had dragged him into great discouragements, the dried air that had seemed to seep into his soul.

He found in Mauritius an interior desert, a difficult passage where everything was arid, but where the hardest remained the lack of perspective. His dream of marrying Eda had floundered on the hard reality of his physical state, which was a handicap to any romantic life.

His passion for architecture was as if locked in captivity, unable to express itself, to deploy its wings, to fulfill itself as a profession.

He felt as if in a dead end, but he had to keep on searching, persevering, and still to go ahead in his quest of a meaning to his life. He felt useless to society, classified among the excluded and marginalized, and the forgotten ones.

His moral suffering was great, and sometimes harder to bear than the pain crisis, which seized his body at times. But, it is in the heart of his suffering that his spiritual journey was going to be defined, without being an escape, but on the contrary a privileged way to go to the essential.

He had lost everything that was linked to happiness: his fiancée, his occupation, his freedom to move, to meet his friends, to go as he wished on the roads of the island; but the happiness that grew in him gradually was not of this world, and surpassed those pleasures and those joys that life can offer here-below.

One of the first fruits of Hyacinthe's spiritual influence was the conversion of his brother-in-law, Arthur, a doctor who belonged to the Swedenborg church, imported in Mauritius by the de Chazal family.

The Swedenborg Church was founded by Emmanuel Swedenborg, born in Sweden in 1688. A scientist by training, he had developed a particular mysticism, expressed in his writings, and spread both in occultism and in freemasonry. Swedenborg's influence had invaded France where he was read by many great authors like Charles Baudelaire and especially Balzac, for whom «Swedenborg summarizes all the religions, or rather the only religion of humanity.»

Arthur belonged therefore to a marginal religious group, more out of tradition than conviction. He searched for truth intensively, and read a lot.

Antoinette, his wife and Hyacinthe's sister, attended Mass early every morning. She left the house on tiptoe, trying not to disturb her husband who was a little upset to see her so much involved in religion. Arthur's conversion was, according to his own view, due to his relationship with the Wiehe family.

Deeply moved by the silent but so edifying example given by Uncle Hyacinthe, and impressed by his mother-in-law's religious zeal and strong faith, he finally asked to be baptized in the Catholic Church.

He was baptized by Monsignor Liston at the Bishopric, and had his mother-in-law as godmother. He then joined his wife every morning for Mass at St-Helen Church, attending the Eucharist with great zeal.

Every time his children accompanied him, they noticed the abundance of tears on the *prie-Dieu* where their father was kneeling, his head on his hands. A young boy, often seated right behind him, observed his great devotion. He had one day said to his mother with emotion: *"He has taken God for himself alone!"*

At Arthur's baptism, Hyacinthe wrote him a letter that showed the caring affection of a brother-in-law, and the gratitude of his patient:

My dear Arthur, I am happy to offer you this 'Imitation of Jesus-Christ', certain that you will appreciate its remarkable pages. Every day I myself find therein a spiritual comfort that helps me, not to bear the trial, but rather to accept it with gratefulness and to give thanks to God for granting me the privilege of suffering.

Receive my affectionate souvenir,

Hyacinthe

This little note says a lot, for it reveals in a few words the quality of Hyacinthe's spiritual life, since he mentioned his suffering as being a privilege, and therefore as a favour, as a kind of spiritual status, as an advantage!

All the advantages he had received through his education and social status seemed secondary, insipid. Material comfort, mundane lifestyles and big projects: all that seemed of a pale colour compared to this Beauty that had seduced him. Riches, honours, health, were nothing in contrast to the wealth he was discovering. This beauty and richness was summarized in the title of the book that was nurturing his soul: 'The Imitation of Jesus-Christ'.

This work, by an unknown author, dates back from the fifteenth century. It had been such a success at the time of its publication that it was for a long time considered the most important book, after the Bible, ever printed in the world. A great number of people have drawn from this work the spiritual food that they were seeking. Saint Therese of the Infant-Jesus, doctor of the Church, wrote in her autobiography: *"For a long time, I sustained my spiritual life by the pure flour contained in the Imitation. This little book never left me, in summer in my pocket, in winter in my muff, I knew almost all the chapters by heart."*

In those pages, when meditating on the life, passion and resurrection of Jesus-Christ, Hyacinthe found the proper words and truths of faith that helped him to better accept the renunciations he had to face.

The first chapters of this work sets the tone:

"The one who follows me will not walk in darkness, says the Lord. These are the works of Jesus-Christ, by which he exhorts us to imitate his conduct and his life, if we truly want to be enlightened and delivered from all blindness of heart. May our main study be therefore to meditate upon the life of Jesus-Christ."

A few lines further, this general orientation is followed by an invitation to detachment, for, as the text says, everything passes here below:

"Vanity in accumulating perishable riches, and in putting one's heart unto them. Vanity in aiming at honours... Vanity in following the desires of the flesh... Vanity in wishing for a long life...Vanity in thinking only of this present life... Vanity in being attached to what passes so fast... Apply yourself therefore to detach your heart from the love of visible things in order to turn it entirely to invisible things."

These few lines reveal Hyacinthe's interior pilgrimage: If he henceforth considered suffering as a blessing, it was not because he had lost his mind, but solely because he understood how much sufferings helped him both to live this detachment which really liberates one, and to better know and love Jesus-Christ, true God.

The sound barrier had recently been broken in the history of aviation. On his bed, Hyacinthe had hurdled another wall in his heart, allowing him to go higher in his spiritual ascension, farther in his search, and to find thereon the joy and the peace promised in the Beatitudes.

During the slow succession of hours and days of suffering, time had seemed endless to him. But now he was getting into a new dimension of Time, the *kairos* or the favourable time, which was offering him the opportunity to live a new quality of relationship with the world and with God. Everything could be accepted and offered in sacrifice.

After having known a kind of purification through the fire of suffering, he understood now that all his life had henceforth to be an only offering, according to the recommendations of Saint Paul Apostle to the Romans:

"I exhort you therefore, brothers, in the name of God's tenderness, to present to Him your body - your whole person – as a living sacrifice, holy, capable of pleasing God: it is here, for you, the just manner of rendering Him a cult. Do not take for model the present world, but transform yourself in renewing your way of thinking so as to discern the will of God: what is good, what is capable to please Him, what is perfect."

All the rest of Hyacinthe's life cannot be understood without taking into account this spirituality, which uplifted him more and more, as his letters thereof can testify.

Eda had to return to the country to take care of her ailing mother. Her stay in France lasted about two years, which allowed her to take some distance and let her wound heal. She would have preferred to remain in France where she received a marriage proposal. But destiny brought her back to Mauritius, where she married Raymond Paturau on the 26th November 1956.

Their union was childless.

Even if this return to the country meant a lot to those who had loved each other so much, Hyacinthe was at peace, and accepted the choice of their separation and of his fresh new vocation.

He had acquired a better frame of mind, with a better inner attitude, and a greater interior freedom. He had been able to forgive the one who had shot him, he had come to terms with his solitude: he had put behind all past joys and did not anymore desperately look forward to heal physically in order to regain them. His whole life was now dedicated to prayer and offering; and a few words resurfaced incessantly from within, like a leitmotiv that helped him to keep faith:

"May Your Will be done".

Father Keenan continued to visit him regularly to bring him the Body of Christ. These moments were of the utmost importance for Hyacinthe. He welcomed the Holy Host with faith, as he acknowledged the real presence of Jesus, his Lord and his God in this tiny piece of consecrated bread. Each communion to the Body of Christ was a great consolation to him. And even if he could not have the Holy Eucharist, he offered his sufferings in union with all masses celebrated around the world.

Mass was for him the Holy Sacrifice above all, the perfect Sacrifice. This word 'Sacrifice' had a real meaning for him, for he had learnt to renounce the world, to offer his life patiently amidst all his tribulations. This experience of self-sacrifice led him to the mystery of Jesus-Christ's cross, to the great gift of the Eucharist, where Christ offers himself with His body given over, and his blood shed.

"What a folly!" he told himself, while testifying the love expressed in the sacrifice of Jesus at the holy Mass! And since mass is celebrated by a priest, he could more and more appreciate the beauty of the priestly vocation.

When his nephew, Adrien, entered the Seminary, he was immensely touched by this event. Adrien was born at Labourdonnais in 1929 when Hyacinthe was only twelve years old. He had seen him grow up in the gardens, and had been attached to him with an uncle's affection.

Hyacinthe wrote to Adrien as he was finishing his formation:

Labourdonnais, 14th October 1949,

My dear Adrien,

I thank you for your letter dated 2 October, which reached me by the last airmail. I am touched by the thought you had of writing to me in spite of all your travel activities: it is I who apologize for not writing earlier, although I intended to do so for a long time. I would like to begin by expressing, at the time that you are starting your philosophical studies, the great admiration that I have for you for having chosen this beautiful vocation that you are now pursuing. I use the word admiration because I know well that, if priesthood is a way that promises us the greatest joys here on earth, this happiness is accompanied by a lot of sacrifices and by a total renunciation.

To the satisfactions and easy pleasures of a worldly life, you have preferred the somehow hard one, but how more beautiful: that of the priest: you will find in it the true happiness, which is working for God.

You can be certain that every day I have a special thought for you in my prayers. May God bless you and grant you His help!

I will perhaps offend your modesty, but allow me in all sincerity to tell you that I am proud of you! Allow me, also, to ask you to say a prayer for me once in a while. Your prayers will be answered more than those of many others.

What I ask of God, you see, is not that He heals my disabilities, or that He returns the impaired faculties that He took back from me, no matter how great may be my desire to recover my health - and it is great, you can believe me! - I have now understood that it is of secondary importance.

I realize more and more the spiritual value of suffering, as much for others as for myself, and what I desire most of all is to be able to accept the Divine Will, whatever it is.

You will understand if I tell you that the sufferings - as much the physical ones as the moral ones - especially in the last few years - and which are still well present today, cannot be truly accepted except with a supernatural help. If, on top of that, God grants me the favour of a cure that science, at the present time, claims to be unable to produce, it will be a great happiness that I do not deserve.

But I realize that by a shortcoming common to all the sick, I have come to talk to you too much about myself. Excuse your old uncle if he shows a tendency to become soft in the head! Or then maybe you will find that my letter is close to a sermon and that I am inverting the roles!

Let us pass then to another subject...."

This testimony illustrates well the good balance within Hyacinthe, who lived in profound unison with God, without for that matter losing neither his sense of humour nor his endearing personality.

He was taking the measure of priestly ministry upon discovering that true happiness consists neither in human fame, nor for what is ephemeral, but in working for God, therefore for what remains eternally,

In a few years, Hyacinthe's life had tipped into another phase, and his inner sensitiveness had developed. He felt things in a new way, not in the way that men usually feel them. He saw the invisible, heard the sweet realities concerning the meaning of this world that comes from God and which goes to God. He touched on essential questions and acknowledged joyfully all the answers received from his faith in Jesus-Christ. Determined, as a true disciple, to follow only one Master, he perceived the role of a priest as the keeper of God's mysteries, holding an incomparable place on this earth. But he felt also, and this was his great consolation, that his vocation as a baptized allowed him to collaborate to the work of God. On rediscovering his baptismal vocation, his vocation to Holiness, he understood better the magnitude of the priestly vocation.

His cousin, Maurice Couve de Murville, the son of Marie Souchon, who had so kindly hosted him in England, was also studying at seminary at this time. Hyacinthe thought of him too, and his self-offering was united to that of the young men who had chosen to dedicate themselves entirely to God. Later, there would be an attempt to develop the fostering of vocations in dioceses, so as to promote the priestly ministry. But Hyacinthe contributed in silence and secrecy, to the hatching of priestly vocation.

Another nephew, Denis, Octave's son, would join the seminary a few years later to be ordained priest in 1969, then later Bishop of Seychelles in 2001.

Even if one cannot necessarily draw a direct relation of cause and effect, it is very probable that the self-offering that Hyacinthe had made on his own initiative became, in the invisible, an effective catalyst to generate an amount of priests and vocations.

In another letter addressed to Adrien, he opened his heart with simplicity and affection:

24 May 1952

Yes, my old friend, I don't forget you in my prayers as you ask me, be assured of that.

If the priestly vocation is the most beautiful one, his task is proportionately the heaviest, if not the heaviest of all. He needs prayers to obtain the graces that are necessary to him. Thank you for thinking of me at your daily mass.

Sometimes infirmity and pains are especially hard to accept but, in spite of those natural reactions, I realize more and more that it is one of the greatest graces that God has granted me."

When the *Foyer de Charité* opened in 1963 at Souillac, in the south of the island, in close ties with Marthe Robin and Father Finet, many Mauritians flocked there to follow spiritual retreats.

Father Mamet, one of the great figures of the Foyer, who led most of the spiritual exercises, often cited Hyacinthe's example, as a model of courage and fruitful faith.

The parallel is undoubtedly audacious but, the benefits that a person like Marthe Robin brought to France and to the world through the offering of herself, in a way Hyacinthe was also secretly bringing them to his native Mauritius.

Marthe testified the trust that dwelt within her:

"As the sufferings increase and get complicated, I feel my confidence become more ardent. Jesus, yes, Jesus, is my sweet and invariable hope. Nothing can separate me from his love."

Hyacinthe did not write notebooks anymore, but what comes out of his few letters look like Marthe's testimony when she had confessed:

"My life is a cross, but a cross of love, a cross of delights, since suffering with Jesus is already not suffering", *"All our sufferings, Jesus shares them."*

"All our crosses, he wants to adorn them with flowers.'

Hyacinthe knew that he owed everything to God and to his close ones, and this certainly had made him grow in humility.

Through his handicap, he felt better suited to chose the last place rather than the first one, and expressed this sentiment with a sense of humour that impressed even more all those who came close to him.

His brothers and sisters were the most faithful ones, after his mother, who was the main support of his life both on the affective and on spiritual levels. She watched over him with a great attention, while respecting Sister's work. She came by everyday to help him, to keep him company, to share news about the ones and the others.

Nature was one of his great consolations, and the stays at Labourdonnais the moments he liked most. Accompanied by his little dog, Titch, he could be seen in full meditation or with a book in front of the pavilion.

Birds continued to come over to greet him, and whilst he was among them, it seemed as if he was talking to them. He listened for a long time to the cooing of the turtledove, contemplated the flowers in the garden and the dances of the trees over the property. As he sensed life bursting all around him he felt in unison with all living beings; he breathed the air abundantly, so happy to be alive.

Among all family members, he showed a special attention towards his nephews and nieces whom he watched growing up. He liked to tease them and to show them his affection, especially on the occasion of their birthdays that he never forgot.

His agenda helped him to keep a record of what life was bringing to him. In it he noted the weather forecast, the books he had read, mails received and sent, prayer intentions, which were entrusted to him.

Every day, without complaint, he offered all his sufferings and his prayers for a particular intention. He tried in so doing to avoid remaining centered on himself, or on the dramas of his life, but rather, smiling and considerate, he chose to pay attention to others and listen to them.

His mother who was also meditating, wrote down in a notebook the fruit of her reflections.

For her also, as for many, Hyacinthe's suffering had inspired her meditation and resolutions.

"Everything comes from God. It is by His grace that we have the desire to improve ourselves.

To offer to God our weakness and powerlessness, to serve and love him as one should. To extract from this weakness the humility which we lack, and to confront ourselves to what God requires of us: renunciations and small sacrifices accepted in a Christian way, till the time comes for us to be examples of patience, and of charity, in everyday life. Confidence in the future, and profound gratefulness for the gifts received, both spiritual and temporal.

To pray with more fervour is my greatest wish. Meanwhile, my soul often lifts itself to God. It is in His goodness that I draw the strength and courage to bear my sorrows.

To thank God every day of my life for the graces He gives me and to ask Him for His help to persevere.

One of my dearest wishes: to do good, as much good as possible, in the measure of my means, and to work more for the salvation of souls, a grace that I shall only receive through prayer. To be an apostle by my example.

My resolution on the threshold of the year 1950 (Holy Year): a lively desire for my sanctification by living a more inward and recollected life.

To be able to achieve that: to be faithful to my meditations and to make them more fervent.

A rule of life that will help me, as much as possible: to have a fruitful time schedule.

In the best of my abilities, avoid the small weaknesses, and possess my soul through patience.

May I have the strength to accept the will of God, and be established in this desire.

Trust in prayer. May God's kindness soothe everything. He directs us for our good, even without our understanding.

Hyacinthe's relationship with his mother uplifted his soul. He prayed more and more, with no interference of hers. She went from place to place with the rosary in her hand. As to him, he had preciously kept the rosary he had received during the war and which had proved such a treasure!

Next to his barometer and a book, one could see that token of piety on his night table. He prayed with it daily, till the day when he offered it to his godson who was leaving for further studies in South Africa.

Labourdonnais - 11 June 1962

My dear Francis,

I trace these few lines in haste, before your departure for Durban. You will find enclosed two small envelopes. One contains a few banknotes, which will help you to choose a very small present. At the present time, I cannot unfortunately do better. At another time I hope it will be different.

The content of the other small envelope will disappoint you perhaps: the rosary, quite ordinary in appearance and make, that is found there, is nevertheless, for me, without any doubt the most precious object that I own till now.

I am happy to offer it to you - on one condition however, that you treat it not as a talisman or an amulet, but with all the respect due to a sacred object. I would even like you to keep it in your pocket. If you do not want it, I would ask you to give it to your father or your mother - or else to any other person who, to your knowledge, will take care of it - Adrien, for instance. If I have held on to this rosary, in this most particular manner, it is because it has its own story, which I relate here briefly:

This is a gift from an army chaplain, Father Arrowsmith-Larkin, around March 1941, in the Sinai desert. The Father had placed it on the Rock of Agony, at Gethsemani, after having blessed it.

Kept in my pocket, or among my effects, it was on me when I was parachuted in France in July 1944.

After having captured me, and put me in a cell, the Germans took it away from me together with everything I had.

One of my guards, an Austrian Catholic, saw it and gave it back to me.

It is the only object that I was allowed to take back with me to England, in September 1944.

Since then it has never left me.

By saying the *'Ave Maria'* every day, Hyacinthe entrusted himself to Our Lady and entrusted to her the hour of his death. He felt intensely that he would not have sufficient energy to live long.

The atmosphere at Labourdonnais had changed owing to the damages caused by the cyclone Carol in 1960, but especially since the closing of the factory that same year.

Hyacinthe realized that everything had an end, and that he had to detach himself even more from the consolations of this world so as to stay always in a condition of preparedness. "*Remain awake*", he read in the Gospels, "*because you know neither the day nor the hour."* Thus, aged 46, he drew up his will. He bequeathed two-thirds of his belongings to Sister, to whom he owed an immense gratitude.

"I chose this way of proceeding in order to conciliate the desire that I have to express my gratitude to Miss Ruscoe for the dedication that she has shown towards me, for about sixteen years."

She, on her side, was contemplating her departure, for she felt she was getting old and worn-out. In fact, she went back to England shortly after.

The remaining third was bequeathed to the Diocese of Port-Louis. In reality, he had never ceased to help the Church, as attested by the receipts he kept in the last pages of his agendas, beside his lists of medication and medical treatments.

He contributed regularly to Amicitia, to his aunt Caroline's community, to the orphanage of Father Margéot, to the works of Father Keenan, and to several other parishes and charity associations of Mauritius.

In total, that added up to 4,000 to 5,000 rupees per year, which represented a large sum at that time.

Solange, who did his housekeeping and laundry, testified, until quite recently, of his kindness and generosity:

"He was a father to me!" she exclaimed.

From a material view- point, the fact of putting down his will was a way to prepare him for death. But since the 11th

November 1953 Hyacinthe had joined the "Our Lady of Good Death" association and was preparing himself on a spiritual level by the promise he had pledged to say several prayers every day, including this one:

"Holy Father, I offer You each and every Mass celebrated or to be celebrated today in the entire Church, in order that, by the blood of Jesus-Christ, Your Son, and through the intercession of the Blessed Virgin Mary, crushed with suffering at the foot of the Cross, You deign to grant to the Justs the great gift of perseverance, to the sinners, the grace of a perfect conversion, and to all who are faithful to Christ, especially myself, my closest ones and the members of the Association, at the last moments on this earth, the reception of the Holy Viaticum, the anointing of Holy Oil, and a death precious to your eyes. Through the same Jesus-Christ our Lord. Amen."

In his "*Song of the Creatures*", Saint Francis of Assisi praises God for death, that he calls his sister. Death is nothing for the one who has prepared oneself to pass the threshold of this phase of life. Hyacinthe was predisposed to that, by accepting to die to himself day after day, by detaching himself from this passing world, so as to attach himself to the One who dwells eternally.

Death is a moment of truth about our life, about our inner dispositions, about our relationship with our neighbour, and about our relationship to God. During his adolescence he had meditated over his father's death.

He was afterwards confronted with the tragic disappearance of his fellows during the war, learning to come to terms with this reality that surrounded him, getting aware that his turn would arrive sooner or later.

He could have died on the battlefield, or disappear incognito at the hospital where he had been admitted. But Providence had allowed him to remain for many years among his own, and he had had time to accept this hour with confidence, to be prepared for it.

The circumstances of his death are astonishing and cast an ultimate light on the mystery of his life.

First of all, his mother left him.

Antoinette died at Labourdonnais, on 30th July 1965, at the age of 88 years, a few weeks before her son. She had supported him till the end in her maternal heart, in her daily prayers, and through her faithful dedication.

She had accompanied him almost to the term of his journey, and could therefore depart in peace.

Antoinette's last words still sound like a testament. Simply three words that sum up what she had sought to pursue and to transmit: *"Prayer, courage, trust."*

Her prayer had constantly irrigated her own life and that of her family. Her courage had allowed her to pass through diverse trials that had dotted her path on this earth. And her trust in God was her strength, her driving force, the secret of her peace and of her happiness.

Because of the sequels of his wounds, Hyacinthe was already quite weakened at the time of his mother's death.

Just like his brothers and sisters he mourned her loss, quite convinced that this separation was but a temporary one, and that it would not be long before he would be reunite to her again.

Labourdonnais was in mourning in the month of August 1965. It was the season of sugar cane harvesting, and everybody was busy, but the atmosphere was different that year. The joy that usually prevailed in the mansion was gone: the pillar of the family was no longer there, and the ones and the others guessed that Hyacinthe would soon leave them too. Indeed, this is what happened on the 9th September of that same year, and maybe this was not a hazard!

On the 9th September 1965, one could read in the local press the accounts of the Constitutional Conference that had opened that very day in London, with Sir Seewoosagar Ramgoolam, the future Prime Minister of the island.

This political event was of an unprecedented nature, since the future of Mauritius was henceforth at stake. The talks had started to decide of the destiny of this colony that had always aroused quite a lot of envy here and there.

At the beginning occupied erratically by the Dutch, but thereafter on a stable basis first by the French, then by the English, its independence was being considered for the first time in its history. This independence was proclaimed on the 12th March 1968. The official deliberations started on the day of Hyacinthe's death.

That being said, the 9th September was above all the day when Mauritians converged towards Sainte-Croix as they still do nowadays.

This pilgrimage was held each year, and Hyacinthe was in unison with it in his thoughts, and especially in his prayers. A huge crowd made its way to the tomb of Father Jacques Désiré Laval, apostle of Mauritius, whose 101th Anniversary of his Entrance in Heaven was being celebrated that year.

Hyacinthe asked to see Arthur, his doctor and brother-in-law, friend and confidant. Unfortunately Arthur could not be reached, having joined all pilgrims brought together by this popular fervour.

Surrounded by a few of his, he thus ended his earthly pilgrimage. He was only 49 years old. An age which in the Bible expresses plenitude: 7 times 7 years. It was the day of the real H Hour, of the great departure, of the ending of an exceptional journey.

He passed away like a self-consuming flame but his heart was burning till the end with a fire of love that accompanied him for his last voyage.

It is said that he had asked for this blessing to die on 9th September, the day of the feast of Father Laval for whom he had a great devotion.

As soon as Eda heard the news, she rushed in to recollect herself in his room, holding in her hand a bunch of pansies, his favourite flowers.

Upon seeing him, stretched out on his bed, smiling, at peace, she wept loudly, nonstop. Not one day had passed without her thinking of him, praying for him, struggling inwardly in order not to reawaken that so strong love that she had always borne him.

But he had been replete by another love that had come to seduce him. He had kept in his flesh the marks of the bullets that had pierced him. But his heart had surrendered itself to the infinite love of God, thanks to which he had tasted the savour of the Beatitudes.

Happy the poor of heart, for theirs is the kingdom of God,
Happy those who cry, for they will be consoled
Happy those who are hungry and thirsty for justice, for they will be satiated
Happy the merciful, for they will obtain mercy
Happy the pure in heart, for they will see God.
Happy the peacemakers, for they will be called Sons of God
Happy those who are persecuted for righteousness, for the kingdom of God is theirs.

Father Laval had personified those verses of the Gospels, and was beatified by Pope John Paul II in 1979. His name still resounds in Mauritius as that of the Saint *par excellence* of the island.

As for Hyacinthe's name, it remained treasured in the memories of those who had been near him, essentially the Wiehe family, and of those who had been frequent visitors of the domain of Labourdonnais.

This property was not accessible to the public till a recent period. Nowadays, visitors can enjoy the beauty of the house and its garden.

One cannot anymore see Uncle Hyacinthe's pavilion that, after his death, had been in use during several years as a meeting room for catechism taught to children of the North School, before being blown off by a cyclone. Nowadays, at this place, a stele has been erected in memory of the one who offered his whole life of suffering in union with Christ, for the glory of God and the salvation of the world.

His testimony was kept in the heart of the family circle for a long time. He is henceforth accessible to all, just like the domain where he lived and where he surrendered his last breath.

After his funerals, Philippe Lenoir wrote in the press:

"A large number of friends and ancient fellow soldiers attended the funerals of Hyacinthe Wiehe who was interred on Friday in the old Pamplemousses cemetery.

(...) On his return to Mauritius, and despite being paralyzed, and oftentimes victim of terrible sufferings, Wiehe was looked after by an English nurse of a remarkable dedication, and was able, when his sufferings allowed him, to put his architectural experience at the service of the firm Boullé-Lagesse-Schaub, where he had very devoted friends. But his condition only got worse and his unbelievable resistance turned the rest of his life into a long Calvary, borne with a human and Christian resignation.

There are some words that one hesitates to use, but may I write without hesitation, that he was a hero, a martyr and a saint.

He died at Labourdonnais, this magnificent property which belongs to the Wiehe since more than a century, in the heart of that same marvellous nature whose beauty conferred him, without doubt, a solace during his merciless Calvary."

In his press article, Philippe Lenoir was calling him a hero, a martyr and a saint. It could be daring to canonize hastily a member of one's family, even if he is considered as such by many.

Only God judges the holiness of hearts. However, he certainly was a hero and a martyr.

A hero is someone who shows courage and exceptional merit. A martyr is a witness of his faith, someone who is ready to reach the ultimate, death if necessary, rather than abjure. Without contest, these two great characteristics can sum up the life of the one who could be a source of inspiration for the new generations.

Hyacinthe had known the Holy Land, in Palestine, during his years of service in the army.

Upon his return, his life was like a seed sown in his native land, contributing to the sanctification of his dear island.

My Dad bears his forename, my Mother wears the engagement ring he had given to Eda before retrieving it at the break-up of their engagement. Every member of the family could claim to be in possession of something that had belonged to him, or a particular memory to share. But above all Uncle Hyacinthe leaves the legacy of a hero and of a witness.

At his death, the founding of the Air Mauritius Company was under way, thanks above all to the efforts of Amédée Maingard, former spy in World War 2, who diversified his activities in the tourism industry. The first flight was expected to take place in June 1967.

Hyacinthe was contemporary to the grand history of aviation that transformed the twentieth century. More and more Mauritians travel nowadays, and everything goes faster henceforth! Progress in the scientific and technical spheres continue to fascinate human beings, to entice them.

In September 1965, television made its faint appearance in Mauritius. The only chain of the island, the M.B.C., broadcasted from 18:30 only and the programs ended with the last one at 20:50. Nowadays, TV channels and packages have been multiplied in the tens.

Those who cannot take the plane spend many hours travelling in front of their TV and their computer. But, what Mauritius needs most to develop, are heroes and witnesses, saints, capable of renouncing everything, to forget about themselves, to enter into a new life dimension, with the strength of faith, the flag of hope and the fire of love. These three virtues come directly from God, and empower fragile beings to draw our world upward, to change society in depth, and to transform history durably.

Faith, Hope and Charity! Here are, in three words, what animated and characterized Hyacinthe's itinerary, what has vivified his whole existence!

Hyacinthe's faith was not an adhesion to a certain doctrine, or to magical formulas. He entertained a living faith, fruit of his personal relationship with Jesus-Christ, and of his perpetual prayer.

He adhered to the Gospel and to the teaching of the Church with his whole being, and he did not hesitate to share that faith whenever the opportunity presented itself.

His journey of faith had drawn him into the theological Hope. Renouncing all hope of a cure, he relied firmly on the promises of his Master, certain to receive the heritage of eternal life. That hope, like an interior anchor, was one of the virtues that he had acquired in a remarkable way and that he encouraged everyone else to acquire.

In one of his letters to Arthur, he said:

"My dear Arthur, I wish to write you a few lines to offer you some very affectionate greetings for your birthday tomorrow. My day will be offered for your sake: May God bless you and grant you hope always! I choose this virtue, but do not dismiss the others."

Herald of faith and hope, Hyacinthe bore witness mainly to a great love, letting that of Jesus-Christ irradiate through him, Christ whom he had sought to follow and imitate to the end, by carrying his cross daily.

The greatest of virtues is love, without which we are nothing. Love is the only luggage that will be carried with us in Heaven. True love is not possessive: it is being shared to the end.

It does not generate bitterness and bears no grudge; it forgives, is sweet and peaceful. It never complains, does not seek its interests, but tries to remain in silent offering. Only Love shall never pass.

Hyacinthe had been baptized on the 24th June 1916, the feast of Saint John the Baptist.

He had received as his first name that of the precursor who said about Jesus:

"He has to grow, and I have to diminish."

Hyacinthe's vocation looks somehow like the saint's. He has prepared the way of the Lord in the hearts of many.

And he will continue to do so.

Postscript

Uncle Hyacinthe has always been venerated by all members of the family, even by the cousins who were still very young then. His enlistment in the armed forces as a parachutist, the history of his wounds just as he landed after the fatal jump in July 1944, his paralysis, his will to face his broken life, all that and much more, supplied him with an aura and aroused in us a feeling of accomplishment, noble and sublime, beyond what is normally expected.

There are, however, many questions still unanswered, and among them, those concerning Uncle Hyacinth's suffering. Then very young, we too had witnessed his suffering crisis following his war wounds; they were uncontrollable and occurred unexpectedly during our visits at his place in his pavilion at Labourdonnais.

Those were my very first contact with great suffering; they aroused in me, at first, a feeling of embarrassment and powerlessness and, later, as I was growing up, numerous questionings regarding my own suffering, and others which I witnessed.

We are all confronted with the problems of suffering and evil.

If we are believers and Christians, this question of suffering is followed by another one: why God, the Creator, the All-Powerful, the good and merciful God, why does he remain without any reaction in the world around us and in our life in particular? Why did He not react to prevent the war, the death and the wounds of millions of human beings?

As Christians, we are called to give a reason to the faith which is ours. We have to try, even if it seems impossible, to reconcile our faith in a God whose infinite mercy we celebrate, and the problem of evil and suffering. To everyone his or her quest, to everyone his or her journey of faith.

For me personally, the first luminous flash in trying to explain what seems unexplainable came from a meditation on Christ's words to the Emmaus pilgrims: "*Wasn't it necessary that Christ endured these sufferings in order to enter into His glory?*" (Luke: 24,26).

From this affirmation of Christ, by successive steps, I came to accept the fact that suffering is an ineluctable dimension of the human condition. By taking our humanity, Jesus suffered too. It is in Him and from Him that all light can come. By accepting the sufferings of life up to the Cross, Christ redeemed humanity and he has made us understand that God is in solidarity with all sufferings and even closer to those who know the greatest sufferings.

At the same time Christ shows us the way we should take to assume our own sufferings.

His resurrection is the definitive victory over evil, suffering and sin, on condition, however, that we accept the way he indicates to us, and that his victory comes to fruition step by step, in each of our lives.

The other more important steps unto this interior path were for me the readings of Francois Varillon: '*The humility of God*', '*Beauty of the World and suffering of men*', and of Francois Varone: '*The Absent God who causes Problem*' and '*This God supposed to love suffering*'. More recently, for a research on the problem of evil and suffering is never completed, the little book of Paul Clavier: '*The enigma of evil or the tremor of Jupiter*'.

As to Uncle Hyacinthe, he had a simple and deep faith He prayed for the war to end rapidly; he visited the Holy Land; he carried with him the rosary that had touched the Holy Calvary; later, he forcefully hoped that the progress of medical science would find a cure for his wounds.

In his condition of great sufferer, in the anguish of a completely blocked human situation, his faith did not waiver and his trust in God remained intact.

More, it is owing to his faith and to his spiritual awareness, sustained by the affection of a family assembled around his mother, herself a person of prayer and of great faith, that he had the force to accept his sufferings without fatalism and without complaint.

Surprisingly, he even came to thank God for his sufferings because they allowed him to make an extraordinary journey of faith and to find 'his vocation' by uniting his sufferings to those of Christ.

While visualizing a broadcast on KTOTV.com, on Fr Pierre Theilhard de Chardin, on 12 October 2015, I was stunned by his testimony regarding his sister Marguerite-Marie, expressed in the preface of her book: ' *The spiritual energy of suffering*'.

Like Uncle Hyacinthe, Marguerite-Marie Theilhard de Chardin was paralysed and bed ridden all her life.

In conclusion to this postscript, here are some extracts from the text of Fr. Pierre Teilhard de Chardin:

" From the point of view of a perfect farseeing observer, and one who would observe the earth for a long time from very high, our planet would appear at first blue from the oxygen that surrounds it; then green from the vegetation that covers it, then luminous - luminous - from the Thought which intensifies at its surface; but also dark - from the suffering which grows in quantity and acuity at the same pace as rises Conscience, in the course of the ages.

Yet the more Man becomes a man, the more the problem of Evil incrusts and aggravates itself - in his flesh, in his nerves, in his spirit – the problem of understanding this Evil and of suffering from this Evil (...)

And it is here that intervenes, in its unequal role, the surprising Christian revelation of a transformable suffering (so long as it is well accepted), into an expression of love and into a principle of union (...) Yes, truly, the miracle, constantly renewed since two thousand years, of a possible "Cristification" of suffering...

"Oh Marguerite, my sister, while dedicated to the positive forces of the universe, I was travelling through continents and seas,

passionately busying myself at observing the surge of all the tints of the Earth, you, unmoving, lying down, were metamorphosing silently into light, in the depth of yourself, the worst shadows of the world.

In the eyes of the Creator, tell me, which one of us will get the better part?"

Denis Wiehe
Bishop of Port-Victoria, Seychelles
Victoria, 31 January 2016